The Six Figure Sales Funnel

The Ultimate Big Profit Customer Keeping Lead Generating Small Business Marketing System

Tanner Larsson

Online Business Systems, Strategies and Development

Editorial Director: Tracy D. Shaw
Cover Design: Lukas Aris
Production and Composition: Digital LowDown

Library of Congress Cataloguing-in-Publication Data

Larsson, Tanner
    Six Figure Sales Funnel: The Ultimate Big Profit Customer Keeping Lead Generating Small Business Marketing System / Tanner Larsson
       p. cm.
    ISBN 1450543650
    1. Selling   2. Success in business   I.Title

Printed in the United States of America.

TABLE OF CONTENTS

INTRODUCTION 7

READY? FIRE! AIM. 7

WHY A MARKETING SYSTEM? 10

YOUR MARKETING UMBRELLA AND HOW IT

INFLUENCES EVERYTHING.................................. 17

MORE THAN JUST ADVERTISING........................... 22

WHY *THIS* SYSTEM?.................................... 29

THE MARKETING FUNNEL SYSTEM:
OVERVIEW 39

PARETO'S PRINCIPLE: THE 80/20 RULE 39

WELCOME TO THE MARKETING FUNNEL 45

BEFORE THEY BUY: YOUR LEAD GENERATION SYSTEM

.... 53

AFTER THEY BUY: YOUR OPPORTUNITY FOR BIGGER

PROFITS AND MORE! 56

ANTICIPATING THEIR NEEDS AND REDUCING SUPPORT

TICKETS 58

THE IMPORTANCE OF TESTIMONIALS AND FEEDBACK 59

ASK THEM FOR REFERRALS AND MAKE IT WORTH THEIR WHILE 60

EXCEED THEIR EXPECTATIONS WITH UNANNOUNCED BONUSES 61

CONSTRUCTING YOUR AUTORESPONDER SEQUENCES......... 63

PREMADE AUTORESPONDER SEQUENCES: BEYOND THE MOUTH OF THE SALES FUNNEL.............................63

KEYS TO AUTORESPONDER SUCCESS......................65

THE PRE-SALES SEQUENCE: WHERE LEADS BECOME CUSTOMERS...69

THE POST-SALES SEQUENCE: BUILDING RELATIONSHIPS, BUILDING PROFITS 71

THE PRE-LAUNCH SEQUENCE: START WITH A BANG! 76

INSTANT OPT-IN SURGE: HOW TO GET QUALIFIED LEADS SUBSCRIBING TO YOUR LIST IN RECORD NUMBERS 79

INTRODUCTION 79

WRITING AND PUBLISHING ARTICLES 81

POSTING TO FORUMS..92

JOINT VENTURES 101

FINDING JV PARTNERS 103

OFFLINE MARKETING 113

IMPROVING YOUR OPT-IN CONVERSIONS 119

FOCUS ON THEM, NOT YOU 121

EMPHASIZE BENEFITS, NOT FEATURES 122

PUSH THEIR EMOTIONAL HOT BUTTONS 126

INCORPORATING PROOF AND BELIEVABILITY 129

THE UNIQUE SELLING PROPOSITION (USP) 135

THE HEADLINE 139

THE MORE YOU TELL, THE MORE YOU SELL 142

WRITE TO BE SCANNED 144

THE STRUCTURE OF AIDAS 146

CONCLUSION 149

INTRODUCTION

> "Learn from the mistakes of others. You can't
> live long enough to make them all yourself."
> —Eleanor Roosevelt

READY? FIRE! AIM.

In his book *The Ultimate Marketing Plan*, copywriter and marketing consultant Dan Kennedy said:

"Personally, I detest planning. I've got the classic entrepreneurial nature—'Ready? FIRE! Aim.' Plan? Geez. Let's just go sell something."

I can certainly relate. That entrepreneurial spirit has always been in my blood, too.

Sure, I had the standard lemonade stand when I was a young child. But I later opened a Pog and Magic card shop in my bedroom at the ripe old age of 11...complete with "flyers" my friends and I passed out at school. Once I cleared my "inventory," it was onto the next project.

During the holidays my sister and I would sell greeting cards and small holiday gifts out of a kid catalogue to our parent's friends and neighbors.

When I saw the older kids selling candy for their school or some other event, I came up with the bright idea to buy a bunch of candy at the store for cheap and sell it at a higher cost at school, earning a profit. That might have worked, except my friends and I ended up eating most of my "profits."

As a young teenager I would attend the local Air Races, and once inside I'd buy the current year Air Race posters at one stand for a lower price, then I would go back to the exits or into the pit area and resell them for a higher price.

During high school while working as a life guard, I also built my own sideline business teaching swimming lessons. I even had a referral system in place where I would give the parent's kid a free lesson for each referral they sent me. It was working out so well that it was affecting the city's own learn to swim program and the city shut me down and prevented me from teaching at any of the city owned pools.

Since then I've sold toys, cars, home services, advertising, electronics, software, hardware, books, info-products, the list goes on.

The Six Figure Sales Funnel

I've held all kinds of jobs, from heavy labor to sales to marketing to management. And through it all, I've always come back to being an entrepreneur.

I've owned several businesses, from part-time "on the side" companies (while holding a "steady" job) to full-time "slit my wrists and pour out the blood" businesses.

To me, there's always been a certain allure to being in charge of your own destiny, even if it means temporarily being a slave to your business.

I suppose I've always been drawn to the "elusive" lifestyle of having more time with my friends and family. More time to spend on leisure activities. More time to do what *I* want to do, and not what some boss tells me I have to do.

I say "elusive" lifestyle, because until recently, the freedom to have more leisure time always seemed just out of reach. But once I learned the strategies and systems used by some of the top marketing insiders, I finally started getting to where I wanted to be.

I should point out that while I did go to college, I didn't study and learn from MBAs and college professors preaching theory. I learned from people who've used these strategies to make themselves a very comfortable lifestyle. In short, I learned from doers.

And by modeling and adapting the most successful systems they've used, I've been able to build my own. But I didn't stop there.

The Six Figure Sales Funnel

Before we go any further, however, let me take a moment to talk about what I'm going to reveal here.

The core content of this book is about your customer/prospect list. It could be a physical mailing list or an email list. I'm going to talk about some ways to build your list, and ultimately I'm going to discuss specific emails you should DEFINITELY include in your email series.

But before I get to all of that, I'm going to start with the bigger picture: the system you use and how the marketing funnel will benefit you once you set it all up. This is important, because many of the concepts I'll cover will have their roots in the marketing funnel concept, which I'll get into.

So, that being said, let's dive into the core concepts...

WHY A MARKETING SYSTEM?

Remember in the movie *Field of Dreams* when Kevin Costner heard the voice whispering to him in his Iowa cornfield, *"If you build it, he will come?"* He built the baseball diamond against all odds, his farm teetering on foreclosure. And in the end the people all came, driven by some desire even they weren't aware of.

Such events make for great fictional stories, but let's face it: when you build your business, people won't flock to it automatically by some unseen force. You have to let them know what you can do for them. In short, you have to advertise.

You need a way to bring in new customers and sell to existing ones. You'd like to have some method to reactivate former customers. You want to try different tactics and strategies and see which ones are the most profitable for you.

There's certainly no shortage of marketing advice out there—some of it good, some of it bad, some that works for some businesses, but not others. In many cases the only way to know for sure is to try them out yourself.

Sure, you want to try the things that have the greatest likelihood of success. Perhaps you attend seminars, try the next new marketing fads, purchase products and services that promise you the world.

You advertise in this publication or that newspaper. You try your hand at online marketing, email marketing. You look at successful sales letters and try to use the best elements for your own campaigns. You network with other professionals, hoping to glean some new ideas to try.

In short, you may be all over the map, trying new methods as well as time-tested ones. Keeping what works and discarding what doesn't.

It's a numbers game, really. Given enough time and money, you'll eventually discover the things that work best for your business. The problem is you can *really* burn through a lot of that time and money before you get there.

Let me offer an example that marketing expert Jimmy D. Brown talks about.

Suppose you approach a car and start pushing it. It doesn't seem to be moving, so you look to your right and see another car, a smaller one that looks like it weighs less and might be moved more easily. So you abandon the first car and start pushing on the second. Meanwhile, another person comes by and starts pushing on the first car you left behind.

After several moments, you realize the second car isn't going anywhere either, and you spot a third vehicle, this one a Jeep Wrangler (those lightweight frames must surely make the Jeep weigh less). So you leave the second car behind and start pushing the Jeep.

Meanwhile, the other fellow is still pushing on the first car. At first it's not moving, just as when you tried to push it. But slowly and gradually, it begins to inch forward. Just a little bit at first. Then it moves a foot. The fellow keeps pushing, and the momentum builds up even further. Now it's moving even faster, covering more distance.

You stop pushing the Jeep to look at the first car moving. Now you're even more determined to get a car of your own moving forward, so you start on a fourth car.

But the first car is really picking up speed now.

The Six Figure Sales Funnel

You're beginning to get frustrated, so you look for lighter cars to push. But you're getting tired. Eventually you decide to call it quits.

When you turn to look at the first car, you notice both the guy and the car are nowhere in sight.

That analogy can be applied to your business as well.

When you spend all your time and money chasing the next greatest thing, you're not able to stay focused on your business and your goals. Yes, some techniques may work for you. It's just not an efficient use of your time and resources.

When you have a plan—a system—in place, you're positioned to grow your business both over the short term and long. That fellow pushing the one car had a plan, simple as it was. And he stuck with it.

Now if he had a tow truck, he surely could've moved it much more quickly and with less effort on his part. But you have to start somewhere, and without that tow truck, you have to make the most out of the resources and ingenuity at your disposal.

And even if every method you tried turned out to be a success, you *still* need some kind of system to tie it all together. It doesn't have to be complicated. In fact, some of the best systems are fairly straightforward. It just has to be consistent and proven.

✓ A system will keep day-to-day tasks from falling through the cracks.

The Six Figure Sales Funnel

✓ Each new strategy that's successfully tested can be placed in the system with the assurance that it will function with everything else already in place and increase the ROI (return on investment) of your system even further. *That means when you start pushing on that second car, your system is still pushing on the first.* This way you'll eventually get <u>both</u> cars moving.

✓ A system removes you from the time-consuming operations tasks and lets you focus on growing your business.

✓ A system lets your business run like clockwork, so you can spend more time with your family or doing the activities *you* enjoy.

✓ Once optimized, your system can be applied to new/other business ventures, with the same expectation of success as your original "seed" system.

✓ Your system can be customized to the needs of your business. The best systems are flexible. They allow you to adapt any aspect of your marketing, and any changes in your marketplace or industry trends.

Let me tell you a story.

The Six Figure Sales Funnel

Several years ago, copywriting legends John Carlton and Gary Halbert were strategizing about their marketing in Gary's office. During their brainstorming session, an employee burst in the room with news that the copier was broken, and there were urgent copies to be made and mailed. Then the computer was down and the phones had been cut off. The landlord was banging on the door for some reason.

So John started folding up his briefcase, thinking they weren't going to get any work done that day.

Well, Gary stood up, pushed the employees out, closed the door, and said, "Let's get back to work."

That's "Operation Moneysuck."

As John puts it: "If you are the guy who brings in the money into your business, then that's your most important job. That's your second most important job, your third most important job, and on down the line."

If you're the one who brings in the money, then that's what you need to be doing. Every hour you spend fixing the phones or the copier or dealing with operations issues is an hour that robs you twice: that hour is gone, and you've spent an hour less bringing in the dough.

A system removes you from the time-consuming operations tasks and lets you focus on growing your business.

The Six Figure Sales Funnel

Stop and think for a moment about how much your time is worth. You really do need to look at your income and break it down to an hourly rate. Here's what each hour is worth to you now:

_____	/ 52	_____	_____	_____
Annual Income	Weeks	/	=	Hourly Worth
	=	Weekly Income	Avg. Weekly Hours Worked	

Here is what you should be thinking about for Operation Moneysuck:

_____	/ 52	_____	_____	_____
Desired Annual Income	Weeks =	/ Desired Weekly Income	= Desired Avg. Weekly Hours Worked	Desired Hourly Worth

...because you have to plan for your goals, not what you're achieving now.

So any task that does not earn you your hourly rate (at a minimum) should be outsourced for cheaper.

Spar

Ultimately that will eventually apply to any task that does not earn you your *desired* hourly rate.

By putting a system in place, you can focus on those activities that will earn you at least your desired hourly rate, while leaving other tasks to your employees or outsourced help.

YOUR MARKETING UMBRELLA AND HOW IT INFLUENCES EVERYTHING

When I get on a plane, I'm glad that pilots use checklists. Even though they're experienced, a checklist makes sure everything is covered and that nothing falls through the cracks. Checklists are proven to work.

Think of a system as a more robust and complete checklist. Whereas the pilot checklist deals with pre-flight testing, the entire system would be the mechanism in which the entire airline company adheres to from end to end.

As an aside, there are basically three ways to grow your business:

1) You gain more customers.
2) You get your existing customers to spend more money with you.
3) You get your existing customers to purchase more frequently.

Note that reactivating old customers that no longer buy from you can be considered a new customer or existing customer, so they would fall into the three methods described above.

So the marketing system, in our case, deals with the end-to-end system of marketing, profit centers, and ROI. Everything that can possibly affect the three ways above to grow your business (and the reverse: keeping your business from shrinking) is part of the marketing system.

To illustrate what I mean, let's do a quick simple exercise. For each role below, put a check next to it if you think marketing should influence that role.

- ❏ The handling of inactive and dissatisfied customers.

- ❏ Customer service

- ❏ Support

- ❏ Human resources: the hiring, firing, and promotions of employees
- ❏ Issuing refunds

The Six Figure Sales Funnel

❑ Product fulfillment

❑ The layout of your business: your store, waiting room, etc.

❑ Appointments and follow-up

❑ Product packaging

Ok, you've probably guessed by now that marketing should influence ALL of those roles. Customer service has a chance to ask for cross-sells, up-sells, and reduce refunds, among other things. The same goes for support. Despite what you may think, the handling of inactive and dissatisfied customers is <u>not</u> the sole responsibility of operations. They are, in fact, opportunities to make more sales and promote referrals. You need to keep your front line service folks plugged in with your marketing campaigns to take advantage of these opportunities.

For example, a department store ran a holiday promotion using full-page newspaper ads, which showcased their increased holiday inventory and price reductions. Their prospects were also offered the easy option to phone in their orders.

Well, when the phones started ringing, the telephone operators knew nothing about their special offer. As a result, customers were unhappy and sales were lost, all because one store manager forgot to tell the telephone operators about the promotion.

Fulfilling product orders sounds like a job for shipping. That may be, but by putting package inserts in with the shipment, you have additional opportunities to sell even more. Your customers just bought from you. They're pleased with their purchase. They've done business with you and they feel good about it. Isn't now a good time to ask for another sale?

How about your store layout? Your waiting room design? Instead of boring magazines and pictures from Sears on the walls, why not plaster your waiting room with photos of past customers and testimonials. The smart car salespeople use this tactic all the time. If you look at their offices, you'll see countless photos of happy customers posing with their brand new cars. Talk about the power of their prospects mentally putting *themselves* in that picture!

Product packaging. A perfect example of this is Stew Leonard's famous supermarket in Norwalk, Connecticut. Where traditional grocery stores would sell upwards of twenty or thirty thousand items, Stew Leonard's focused on one of their specialty niches: freshness. They carried only two-thousand items.

Every day they brought in fresh fish, cleaned it up, nicely packaged it, and proudly displayed it in their freezer cases, labeled "FRESH FISH."

Now Stew Leonard's was a store that wisely listened to their customers, and when sales of the fish weren't as high as they had hoped, they turned to their customers to find out why and what they wanted.

Well it turned out that it was a perception issue. Their customers told them they wished Stew Leonard's carried *real* fresh fish, like the ones on slabs of ice at the farmers' market. So the store started packaging the fish in two different ways: 1) the way they always had, and 2) unpackaged on a slab of ice in a small display unit with a sign reading "Fresh Fish Market."

Their results? Sales of fresh fish more than doubled, proving that how they packaged their fish was at least as important as the other factors involved.

What about appointments and follow-up? Issuing refunds? These are all opportunities to sell even more. No opportunity should go untapped. And your marketing system should reflect that.

And if you think Human Resources should be left with all the hiring and firing decisions, think again. Even a dishwasher or busboy plays an integral role in the business of a restaurant. Whether or not they interact directly with customers is irrelevant. Your customers still see the results of their actions.

There's an old story about a janitor who worked for NASA in the seventies. One day upper management was giving a tour to some government officials, who were evaluating the funding that NASA needed. They stopped and asked the janitor what he did for NASA.

"I helped put a man on the moon," the janitor replied.

The Six Figure Sales Funnel

It's that kind of mindset that you absolutely must instill in your employees if you want to make sure your business is positioned for growth. All roads must eventually lead back to marketing. Why? Because it's the only way your business will grow. Your "marketing umbrella" needs to touch all aspects of your business.

MORE THAN JUST ADVERTISING

Your marketing is more than just having great ads and sales copy. No matter how great your ads are, there are other factors that come into play to determine how successful your business will be. Your marketing system needs to cover all of them.

It's been said that there are generally three things that determine how successful your marketing campaign will be. In order of importance, they are:

1) Your market
2) Your offer
3) Your sales copy or ads

Notice that your ads are the *least* important of the three?

It makes sense when you think about it. You could have the greatest ad for an expensive set of golf clubs in the world. But if you show that ad to a group of literature buffs, it ain't gonna cut the mustard.

If, however, you have a weak ad and you target a hot market who wants what you're selling, you'll do much better than a great ad targeting a weak market.

Likewise, your offer has to be good. I would say even great—a "no-brainer." If your golf clubs ad is great and you target your ad to die-hard golfers who know, trust, and purchase your clubs, you're not going to make many sales if they can get the same set of clubs at their local golf store for less. Unless there's a compelling reason to buy them from you instead.

So even though you've got a good ad targeted to the right market, if your offer is weak it doesn't matter that you hired the best copywriter in the world to write your ad: it's still not gonna sell.

Only when all three work together—your market, your offer, and your copy—do you make the maximum sales possible.

I would even add two more success factors to the other three, the first being media costs.

You already know what your product costs you. And you know your gross profit margin, based on the cost in which you sell that product. For example, if you have a 75% margin on a $100 product, your product would cost you $25 to produce or obtain, and your gross profit will be $75 per item sold.

The Six Figure Sales Funnel

In addition to the cost of the product, you also have fixed costs, but these too are known in advance. So the unknown variable is really the cost of your media.

If you buy a full-page ad in a national magazine and it costs you $18,000, and you earn a gross profit of $15,000, you are short the $3,000 necessary to cover the cost of the ad and break even. So the ad is considered a failure as a result. But if you're able to obtain that same full-page ad for $10,000, then you make a profit of $5,000, and the ad turns into a success.

In this example, the difference between success and failure is how cheaply you can buy your media.

Note that I'm assuming you're running your best copy—your control ad. Improving the response rate of the ad can also make the difference between success and failure, but all things being equal, you can see the direct result of your media costs on your campaign.

Now perhaps your full-page ad in that particular magazine may not bring a positive ROI if you can't get the space cheap enough, but it may in another magazine or another *media*.

For example, direct mail has no media costs— just printing, postage, and list rental, if applicable. The same can be said of catalogs. Those costs are fixed, especially if you are mailing to your own "house" list.

However...print display ads, TV, radio, and any other negotiable medium introduces variable costs that could impact the success or failure of your marketing campaign.

I'll share with you some great ways to save quite a bit of money in media costs in a later section.

The other success factor I'd add to the "standard three" is timing. Timing is arguably part of the offer/market match, but results can swing in a huge arc between more successful and less successful, even though they may still be within the range to be considered an overall success. In fact, the best market/offer match-up is often "tuned" to the timing of the ad being run. That is, what will the market bear? Often it should be the other way around: the ad should be mailed/run/aired when the timing is at its most opportune moment to generate the highest profits and ROI.

The timing factor is especially evident when tying in promotions to certain current events in the news. Often the news hits with little warning, and you have to act fast to develop and deploy the promotion while the news is still fresh. Obviously events that stay in the news for longer periods give you more time to plan, but it's still better to be first.

Even better is when you know news is coming, and you plan for all outcomes in advance. There's a reason sportswear and other companies have promotions ready to go for both teams in the Superbowl or World Series. One of the two teams will win. How else could they start their campaigns the *minute* the official results are known?

The same could be said for elections. How about the release of a movie or music CD? An upcoming holiday. A NASA mission. The passing of a new law. The Olympics. Any time you have an opportunity to use the news for your benefit, you should strongly consider it. This is especially important when you send a broadcast email to your list. Why should they open yours in a sea of others?

You should know that the 2 most important factors (in order of importance) that the people on your list consider when deciding whether to read your email are:

1. **Who the email is from.** Changing your "From" name often or from what they're used to seeing can hurt your open rate.

2. **Your subject.** And if they DO open your email and feel "suckered" because your subject has nothing to do with the content, they will likely delete it instantly, taking no further action. More on that in a bit…

And those 2 factors will determine whether they:

1. Open your email

2. Delete your email without opening it

3. Not delete it, but save it for later

Obviously we want them to take the first action: to open your email immediately, where your copy takes over and convinces them to take the desired action.

But back to "entering the conversation already in their minds." Whenever there is an event they are already talking about, you should use that to your advantage. And if that event can result in different outcomes, planning for all possible outcomes is just one way you can be among the first.

And speaking of being the first, there's another aspect of timing that we're going to cover in the sections ahead. "Conventional" wisdom tells us that if there are a lot of products similar to yours being sold to your target market, there is usually a demand for your product as well.

Well there's also an opportunity to dominate your niche market by introducing a product that is harmonious with their desires and needs, and where you are the first to market such a product to them. However, like any other marketing strategy, there is a risk-to-reward ratio involved. By being the first, you are taking more risk, but you will also reap more reward if successful. But the reverse is also true: you run a greater risk of losing more if it's a failure.

The Six Figure Sales Funnel

The way we limit this risk is by *testing*, which allows us to determine whether to move forward, or "roll out," with our promotion or cut our losses short. So as you can imagine, testing is performed on a much smaller scale on a sample representative of our larger market. We'll cover testing in greater detail later on.

But…getting back to your market, your offer, and your copy. The three together will generally determine the success of your marketing campaigns. That's why great ads alone won't grow your business.

You need to factor in the other things that will make or break your success. A good marketing system should incorporate all of this as well—consistently—from end-to-end.

One of the greatest systems ever developed in the fast food industry was Ray Kroc's vision of consistency, based on a proven formula that was to be applied to all McDonald's restaurants.

McDonald's didn't start out as an empire. It was Ray's system, based on the fact that McDonald's restaurants in California had the same menu prepared in the same way as the McDonald's in New York, that enabled their tremendous growth.

Ray developed a system that he tested and tweaked, until it was a model of success: his "seed" system. Then he multiplied that system in a huge way, rolling it out on a grand scale and taking the rewards that came with it.

The Six Figure Sales Funnel

The beauty of this concept is anyone can do it, whether on a large or much smaller scale, and get the same results as the "seed" system.

I hope I've convinced you about the merits of putting a system in place for your marketing. More than likely you already have some kind of general system or plan working for you, even if it's not complete or consistent. You may know what needs to be done, but maybe you're not sure how to go about it. Or maybe you're just shifting your focus week-to-week, month-to-month, chasing down the methods that you think will give you the greatest success at that time.

But opportunities *are* slipping through the crevices you're not watching. That car you're pushing just isn't moving forward fast enough.

Let's face it: you've been down that road before. Isn't it time to focus your efforts on what's <u>really</u> important to you and your business?

I'm here to help you do just that.

WHY *THIS* SYSTEM?

The short answer? Because it works. But to answer that question more fully, let me tell you how this system came to be.

I didn't invent the core concepts. The system is based on proven marketing principles honed over the course of time by successful entrepreneurs…the doers, the testers, and the business builders. They are the ones who've built their businesses from scratch and lead the way to turn these businesses into multi-million dollar empires.

After high school when I ventured out on my own to create my first business; a window cleaning business, I was a bit perplexed on how to go about my marketing, since I didn't have the deep pockets of large corporations. I started reading about successful entrepreneurs who built their businesses from the ground up, and I was especially interested in some of the creative ways they marketed in the early days on a shoestring budget.

In particular, I was fascinated by direct response marketing, especially in the mail order industry. Here were ads for products that you couldn't pick-up, touch, or examine, yet people would send checks off to far away places, only to wait several weeks to receive the goods they ordered.

Now mail order certainly wasn't new to me. I grew up reading Sports Illustrated and other magazines that carried lots of direct mail ads.. Gary Halbert and other notable copywriters at the time had a virtual monopoly on my eyeballs. And as I grew older, it was a major event when my Agora Publishing subscriptions arrived in the mail.

So while mail order itself wasn't new, I was looking at it from a different perspective. As I read more about mail order and direct response, I realized that seasoned direct marketers would make better mentors to me than big business marketing departments or ad agencies. The seasoned pros have been through the trenches. They've seen what worked extremely well and what didn't work. They rolled out their successes and learned from their failures. They carefully measured their results to the penny. Anyone without this real-world experience can only guess at what's going to work. And naturally I wanted my business to be successful. Guessing was simply not an option for me.

I didn't realize it at the time, but by adapting the premise of a two-step ad (where someone gives you their name and address to request more information about your product—the first step—and you then follow-up by sending your marketing materials—the second step), I was well on my way to establishing my first lead generating system. At the time (nearly 20 years ago), this was a big breakthrough for me. But it was just the start.

A few years later, I started learning from a fellow by the name of Lawrence Tabak, who was a student of Gary Halbert at the time. In particular, I admired Lawrence's "no nonsense" style and his ability to show in a straightforward manner how easy it was to sell a product via mail order in the most efficient and cost-effective way. I also began to learn how to write compelling direct response copy.

The Six Figure Sales Funnel

That year I launched my first mail order product, which was a "how to" book on making money on eBay. It wasn't a bad campaign for my first. I made a slight profit, but more importantly I learned a lot from actually *doing* it, rather than just studying it. I learned firsthand about list brokers and rented my first lists. I learned about testing and tracking my campaigns. And I learned about copywriting and creating info-products.

I'm also a little embarrassed to say that I used a two-step ad in some places where a one-step ad was really warranted, plus other mistakes, but that was part of the learning process.

I dabbled a little more in mail order, but eventually focused my efforts back on my window cleaning business. The business was doing quite well, and I was making a good living from it. I continued to study successful entrepreneurs and adapt their best strategies in my business. As a result, my business grew at a steady clip and continued to grow for many years.

Fast forward to the present. I continued to build and adapt my system over the years and used it successfully to start two other businesses in the home services niche both of which earned over 6 figures in the first year (one of them actually earned 6 figures in a little over 60 days).

A few years later I sold all my businesses and dove headfirst into Internet marketing and online sales. I had a web design business for while, and eventually turned to marketing consulting.

The Six Figure Sales Funnel

I discovered that many of my clients had no real marketing system in place and flew by the seat of their pants (you might be surprised at how many).

So a big part of the value I provided was helping them to put a solid marketing system in place that let them focus on the core aspects of their business. At the same time this system would help to reveal underexploited profit centers and encourage the growth of their business.

Best of all, it can easily do the same for you.

✓ It's based on other systems that have been proven to work for their respective businesses...systems that are quietly making their owners fortunes in profits and business growth.

✓ It's been crafted to work for practically any business.

✓ It's adaptable. You'll be able to insert your own steps, as well as the methods used by your coaches and mentors.

✓ It contains little known strategies and tactics used by the top moneymaking doers.

✓ It's designed so you can focus more on the methods that give you the best results.

✓ You can start getting results right away, while still employing strategies for long-term growth.

✓ You can start it on a shoestring budget or a larger investment (plus use the 'ol time versus money tradeoff).

The system itself is fairly straightforward, but it's *how* you get leads, *how* you follow-up, *how* you sell that's really going to make the difference between barely making it work or a windfall of profits and growth. And I'll take you step-by-step through this process.

Is this the "best" system or the only system you should use? That's a highly personal choice, and a decision you'll have to make. I wouldn't think of it in those terms, but rather once you have a chance to put it to the test, ask yourself: "Is it working for me?" I would say keep an open mind to everything, but keep only those methods that you or someone trustworthy has personally tested and found to be successful. As President Reagan used to say, "Trust, but verify."

Renowned dealmaker and business growth consultant Jay Abraham had a client in the construction business. This company would deliberately breakeven on the first job they performed for a new client. And they made sure the client knew that fact. It was their way of showing their quality and performance. As a result, 80 percent of those clients hired them again, adding $50 million a year to their bottom line.

Another of Jay's clients brings in $6 million a year performing maintenance and repair work for air-conditioning and heating. Twice a year that company does a mailing to all their clients, and they also advertise a $19.95 tune-up and cleaning service. Although it actually costs them $30.00 to perform the service, they end up making money instead of losing it. That's because about half the people they visit end up having an immediate problem that needs to be repaired—a problem they weren't aware existed. And that problem adds a minimum $125.00 profitable service charge that they collect right there and then. So even though they lose about $10.00 on the initial service, they know before even heading out to perform the service calls that they'll make a nice profit overall.

On top of that, 50 percent of their new clients having the service performed for the first time end up being regular customers, bringing in an additional $2.5 million a year.

Do you think there are opportunities to sell one of your entry products or services at a loss or breakeven to make even more on the back end?

Legendary copywriter John Caples once tested the following two headlines of an ad to see which one gave the greater response. Can you guess which one was the winner?

The Six Figure Sales Funnel
"What Would Become of Your Wife If Something Happened to You?"

"Get Rid of Money Worries for Good!"

You see, no matter how experienced a marketer you are, it's nearly impossible to precisely guess what the market wants or will respond to without testing. John knew this, hence his test. By the way, the second headline out pulled the first, even though an advertising jury (think professional focus group) favored the first to win.

The famous New York merchant John Wanamaker once quipped, "I know 50 percent of all my advertising is being wasted, I just don't know which half!" With testing and tracking, he would have known.

Do you want to know which of *your* ads are earning their keep and which ones you should ditch? Would you like to learn the right way to test?

Online marketers John Reese and Yanik Silver have both mastered building customer loyalty. In fact, if you've spent any time marketing online, you're probably well aware of John's record-breaking $1.08 million in sales within the first day when he sold his *Traffic Secrets* course in 2004.

Yanik has had equally great success with his courses, seminars, and other products. John and Yanik both use many secrets to maximize their profits, but I think one of the biggest reasons for their success has been the way they developed their customer loyalty and built social proof around their brand identities (i.e. themselves). And they have a solid system for duplicating that success in all of their endeavors.

Plus—and here's a big one—neither of them restrict their marketing efforts to online only. That's an important distinction between most Internet marketers and these pros. And one of the reasons they're so successful.

Would you like to build that kind of customer loyalty and social proof? Do you think your business will benefit from both online and offline marketing…a form of hybrid marketing that contributes more as a whole than either one could alone?

Joe Sugarman may be famous for his BluBlocker sunglasses line, but long before he entered the retail market, Joe was a veteran of direct response and the mail order business, selling gadgets and high-tech products to the mainstream. Joe applied his tested direct marketing methods to the infomercial media, and he was also among the first to use toll-free numbers to take orders via credit cards. His competitors, of course, imitated his methods whenever they could because they worked. Given the opportunity, why do you think they copied Joe instead of some high-priced MBA consultant or ad agency?

These are all real examples of marketing veterans in the trenches making *billions* for themselves and their clients. Does this mean every attempt was a success for them? Did everything they touched turn to gold? Of course not. They all had their share of disappointing results and failures too. All the more reason for you and me to learn from them and ethically "steal" their ideas.

So with that said, let's progress to the fundamental concepts of this marketing system: the *80/20 Rule* and the *marketing funnel*.

THE MARKETING
FUNNEL SYSTEM:
OVERVIEW

> *"Timid salespeople have skinny kids."*
> —Zig Ziglar

PARETO'S PRINCIPLE: THE 80/20 RULE

In 1895, Italian economist Vilfredo Pareto wrote about a mathematical formula he discovered modeling the distribution of wealth in his country and every other country he studied. Pareto observed that twenty percent of the population owned eighty percent of the land. Eventually others found similar distributions that applied to their own situations. Dr. Joseph Juran, a quality management expert working in the US in the 1930s and 40s recognized a universal principle he dubbed the "vital few and trivial many."

As a result, Juran's observation that 20 percent of something is responsible for 80 percent of the results became known as Pareto's Principle, or the 80/20 Rule.

The 80/20 Rule simply means that in any situation, a few (20 percent) are vital and many (80 percent) are trivial. Put another way, the 80/20 rule states that the relationship between input and output is rarely, if ever, balanced. In Pareto's case it meant 20 percent of the people owned 80 percent of the wealth. In Juran's case he discovered that 20 percent of manufacturing defects were causing 80 percent of all problems. You can apply the 80/20 Rule to almost anything.

In fact, 20 percent of your staff and colleagues probably give you 80 percent of all the support you need. Don't take them for granted, because true advocates like them are rare. You probably read trade journals and books, and I'll bet 20 percent of them supply 80 percent of your knowledge in those subjects.

And what about those jobs around the house that you've been meaning to get around to doing? The 80/20 Rule means that that if you have a list of ten items to do, two of those items will turn out to be worth as much or more than the other eight items put together.

The 80/20 Rule can be harnessed in many ways for your business. And when I say 80/20, that's really an

The Six Figure Sales Funnel

approximation. Sometimes it might be 70/30, sometimes 85/15, you get the idea. The crux of the concept is that a small amount of something is responsible for the vast majority of results.

Even how you spend your time is subject to the 80/20 Rule. Ever notice that 20 percent of your efforts is responsible for 80 percent of your success? And the reverse is also true: 80 percent of your efforts is only responsible for 20 percent of your success.

Look familiar?

You're in the 80 percent (the less desirable) segment of your efforts if...

✓ You're working on tasks that aren't in your area of expertise.

✓ You're spending time on tasks other people want you to do, but you get little or nothing in return.

✓ You're doing a lot of prep work that's setting you up for the "real" work.

✓ Tasks are taking much longer than you thought they would.

✓ You're frequently putting out fires and working on "urgent" tasks.

✓ You're not happy, you're complaining, or you don't feel a sense of accomplishment upon completion of your tasks.

However, you're in the 20 percent (the more desirable) segment of your efforts if...

✓ You're outsourcing or hiring people to do the tasks outside your area of expertise or ones you prefer not to do.

✓ You're engaged in activities that help to advance your purpose and achieve your goals.

✓ You're knocking out tasks quickly, especially the "core" work that needs to be done.

✓ You're doing things you enjoy and feel good about.

✓ You may be working on tasks you don't like, but you're doing them knowing they contribute to the bigger picture.

✓ You're happy, smiling, and you feel a deep sense of accomplishment upon completion of your tasks.

The Six Figure Sales Funnel

So how does the 80/20 Rule apply to the marketing funnel? And what is this funnel anyway?

First, the 80/20 Rule. You're probably aware that 80 percent of your income is determined by 20 percent of your customers. If that's not the case, then you are likely missing out on a *lot* of profitable opportunities. Let me explain.

If your customers contribute to your profits on a one-to-one ratio (1:1), then that means your business model is set up so that once a customer buys from you, you never sell to them again. One opportunity. One sale. End of the line. Time to move on to the next customer...

But if you continue to sell to them again and again, you'll ultimately discover that there are certain customers who will buy more often and spend more money with you over the long haul than others. Some will still buy once, and you'll never hear from them again. That's fine. It's going to happen no matter what system you have in place.

But your system will play a major role in determining what those top "20 percenters" will ultimately spend with you. And whether you have a top 20 percent to begin with.

These folks are your "A" clients, your "A" customers. They're the ones you want to treat like royalty. Just like the 20 percent of your staff and colleagues who are true advocates for you, your "A" customers are true advocates for your company. And they show their loyalty by purchasing from you, and by referring your business to others.

Let me give you an example that illustrates just how powerful referrals can be.

I recently started a referral program for my consulting business. In the first *two weeks alone*, I had over $23,000 in new business sent my way. All by referrals. And that doesn't even count the joint venture partnerships in the works, where I expect the real business to come from.

So the system you want to employ should have a built-in bias towards encouraging your customers to:

✓ Make bigger purchases with cross-sells and up-sells.

✓ Purchase more often.

✓ Graduate towards making bigger ticket purchases, those that give you greater and greater profits.

✓ Become an advocate for your business and refer others to you.

The system should also provide a strong incentive, an "ethical bribe" if you will, for the people in your target market (i.e. your prospects) to raise their hands and become your leads. Willingly and voluntarily.

WELCOME TO THE MARKETING FUNNEL

In college I had an adjunct marketing professor whose day job was as a Marketing strategist for a Fortune 500 company. Through his direct knowledge I learned about brand building and marketing to the masses. Large corporations like that often use what's called the "open house," or brand-building, model of advertising, which is expensive, time-consuming, and requires a lot of brand equity and trust over time before people make decisions to buy from them.

With the "marketing funnel" model, a person makes a small purchase (yes, supplying an email or physical mailing address is considered a payment of sorts), and over time you "funnel" your customers towards more and more high-end products and services, step by step, by selling them to the next level.

The two are entirely different business models, and they both work in their own ways. For most entrepreneurs, however, the brand-building model is too cost-prohibitive and time-consuming to use by itself, involving many resources that simply aren't practical. That doesn't mean you shouldn't use it within your means. In fact, you'll soon see how to incorporate both the open house *and* marketing funnel models in your system (for starters…we're just getting warmed up!).

So by "funneling" (others call it "backending" or "up-selling"—Dan Kennedy calls it "gathering the herd") your prospects into paying customers, you're setting the stage to provide tremendous value to them. So much value, in fact, that your customers begin to look forward to receiving content from you. And with that value comes the opportunity to take your customer to the next level, where you can sell higher-end goods to them.

And this isn't a one-sided benefit. Both you and your customer benefit by this relationship. Your customer benefits when he gets even more value…something he really wants. You're helping him in that regard. And of course you benefit as well by slowly graduating your customer to your "A" list, where you can provide even more value.

I once knew a salesman from a large workforce management company. This company sold expensive computer systems that helped call centers forecast their incoming call volume, determine how many customer service people they needed to handle those calls, and even generate the most efficient schedules for those reps in order to maintain a desired level of service.

This guy was an old pro when it came to managing his leads. When a potential client company would issue a request for proposal to him (basically an opportunity for his company to provide a quote based on the issuing company's needs), he would keep track of all the people involved in the decision-making process, plus any supporting personnel. Basically anyone's info he could get his hands on.

Now when he learned that a key person moved from one company to another (which was fairly common), and that new company was in the market for his product, he would personally contact his "lead" from the old company (now working for the new one) and continue his funneling efforts there, while still maintaining the funnel at the old company.

Now imagine he was doing this for all of his leads, wherever they ended up. He had funnels in place everywhere. Do you think he had skinny kids?

Personally I think every sale he made was well earned. Anyone who can keep track of all those funnels and people hopping companies deserves to earn a profit.

Figures 2-1 and 2-2 (pg 47) show the typical marketing funnel. Figure 2-1 shows an offline version of the funnel model, and figure 2-2 shows the online equivalent. Note that the only differences are at the top of the funnel, signifying the manner in which you obtain your leads. Online they visit your website before they supply their information and become a lead. In the offline world, they would receive your offer in some other manner.

A truer representation might represent your target market as *suspects*, who become prospects only after raising their hands (i.e. they become your prospects when they become your leads), but however you view them, the goal is to obtain leads, where you will then attempt to convert them into paying customers.

Notice how the width of the funnel gets smaller towards the bottom? The width represents the number of customers at that height, or stage, of the funnel. However, the smaller the width, the more money they are spending with you. In fact, the amount of money they spend with you can be thought of as being inversely proportionate to the width of the funnel (more or less). So the 20 percent responsible for 80 percent of your profits are at the bottom of the funnel. The other 80 percent that give you 20 percent of your profits are towards the top. This distribution is a general observation and not a mathematical absolute. As I mentioned earlier, it might be 70/30 or 90/10 or somewhere in between.

This is no accident. Your "A" customers, your biggest advocates, are in the smallest segment of your customer base…the bottom of the funnel (but the top in terms of the value you deliver to them).

The Six Figure Sales Funnel

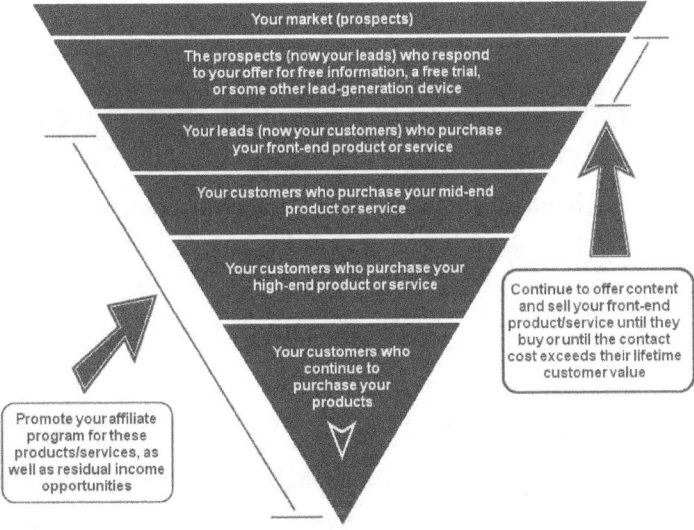

Figure 2-1 The Marketing Funnel (Offline)

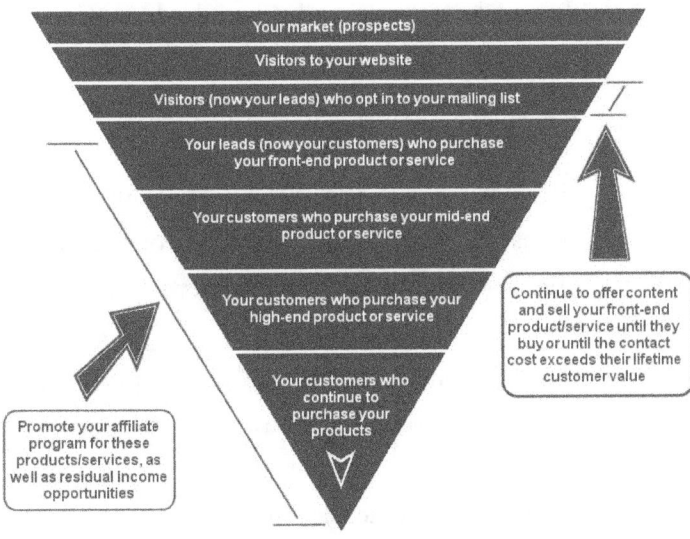

Figure 2-2 The Marketing Funnel (Online)

The Six Figure Sales Funnel

Let's walk through each step of the funnel to gain a clearer understanding of how the funnel works.

1) Your prospect enters the funnel by responding to your incentive or "ethical bribe" to raise their hand and give you their contact information. He is now a lead on your mailing list.

2) You continue to provide value to him, but you want him to make the transition from a non-paying lead to a paying customer. As a result, you give him a front-end, or entry-level, offer on a product or service directly related to the value he received when opting to join your list. You may make the offer at a breakeven or even an initial loss, because you know you will more than make up for it on back-end sales.

3) If he doesn't purchase your front-end product, you continue to sell him on the same offer or different front-end offers—ideally both, because he just may not be in the market for your initial offer at this time, but may be later.

4) When he purchases your front-end product, he is now a customer. You are now "warming him up" to doing further business with your company. Once he sees that you over deliver on

The Six Figure Sales Funnel

your promise of value, he'll feel more comfortable buying from you again.

5) You want to graduate him to the next price level, so you make him an offer on a higher-end product or service related to the entry-level one he already bought. If he doesn't buy, you follow a similar approach as step 3 above. That is, you continue to make him offers, but this time on the mid-level product.

6) Once he purchases your mid-level product, you move onto the high-end product. He is now conditioned to buy from you with confidence and without worry, because he knows what an outstanding value you've been giving him. He's seen the results of your products first hand, so his buyer's resistance is reduced. He is now on his way to becoming one of your "A" clients, the 20 percent responsible for 80 percent of your profits.

7) You continue to sell him higher ticket items and provide even greater value to him.

The steps I have listed are a very simplified approach. You'll soon see that there is much more to it if you truly want to be successful in the long run, but it's not rocket science by a long shot.

The Six Figure Sales Funnel

For instance, each time he purchases from you, you'll want to do up-sells and cross-sells. Up-sells are more expensive finishes, grades, styles, or a bigger version of the product ("Do you want to super-size that?"). Cross-sells are other items that go along with the product. Something complementary. A carrying case, extra paper, ink, blank media, whatever ("Do you want fries with that?")

After he buys, you'll want to ask him for referrals, a testimonial, and do everything in your power to make sure he is satisfied. You want him to be satisfied so he'll buy again of course, but you want also want to reduce your refund rate and gain his endorsement. You want him to tell all of his friends and colleagues about his positive experience with your company.

You probably know when someone has a bad experience with a company they're more likely to tell others about it than when they have a pleasant experience. You want to encourage them to tell all about their pleasant experience.

And then you'll want to develop some kind of residual income, where they pay you so much a month or year forever until they cancel. Not everyone will do that, of course, but your "A" customers probably will. And you can create different residual levels, just like you have different product levels, all at different price points.

BEFORE THEY BUY: YOUR LEAD GENERATION SYSTEM

There are primarily 2 methods we're going to discuss today to get your prospects to sign up for your list.

1. You offer something of value that they will get when they opt-in to your list.

2. You give them valuable content up front, then let them know they can sign up to your list for even more. Also known as the "reverse" opt-in.

Ideally, you'd like to do both of them. Especially in markets like the crowded Internet Marketing (IM) niche, prospects have become increasingly skeptical and reluctant to provide their email address. The reverse opt-in is designed to put them at ease by showing them up front some of what they'll be getting.

In both cases, you want them thinking, "Wow! If this is what he's giving away, I'd like to see what he's selling!"

Let's take a look at some proven lead-generation devices from my good friend, John Ritskowitz's, product.

On the main sales page;
(http://www.copywriters-toolkit.com), you'll notice he offers a "sneak preview" in his 3rd P.S., where they can

get his Profit DNA book and some of the tools in the toolkit just by signing up for his list.

We've also tested the following various squeeze pages (pages where the sole purpose is to "squeeze" your name and email address out of you).

The first 2 are notification pages, designed to "sell the mystery" and get them on the early bird list. After each link below, I've also listed the conversion percentage (the percentage of people who signed up to be on the list).

- http://www.copywriters-toolkit.com/index-d.html (22.03%)

- http://www.copywriters-toolkit.com/index-r.html (24.82%)

- http://www.copywriters-toolkit.com/read.html (14.56%)

- http://www.copywriters-toolkit.com/dna.html (14.87%)

There were others, but these performed the best. As you can see, "selling the mystery" (the first 2 listed above) is an important concept that shouldn't be overlooked, whether a pre-launch or not!

The Six Figure Sales Funnel

Now for Johns reverse opt-in. We created a book called *"The Profit DNA: How To Unlock The Code To Maximum Profits Through Self-Evolving Websites."*

In it, we placed strategic links to his salesletter and (at the time the book was released) the various squeeze pages that we were testing.

Just be careful not to overdo this. You don't want your book to be a pitch-fest. You want it to provide valuable content that people would actually pay for, and then add as almost an afterthought, *"Oh, by the way, you can learn more about X here..."*,

This is not rocket science. Perhaps you already know many of these tactics, but let me ask you, how many of them are you *using* right now?

Don't feel bad. It takes time to get them all into place. I've spent the better part of a year getting many of my puzzle pieces into place (in my defense, I've been very busy working on my clients problems...they ALWAYS take precedence over my own projects).

The point is, though, I'm giving you this info as a way to shortcut your own efforts here, because it's THAT important!

I promised you the "meat" in this book, and aside from some of the introductory concepts I needed to review about the marketing funnel and a little bit about my background, we're going to skip over the fluff from here on out.

The Six Figure Sales Funnel

I could talk about lead generation all day, as there are many ways to do it successfully. But I think I've covered the important concepts.

AFTER THEY BUY: YOUR OPPORTUNITY FOR BIGGER PROFITS AND MORE!

After they've already purchased your front-end product, your work is not done. At least, not if you want more profits, testimonials, feedback, customer loyalty, referrals, and more.

Let's begin with *more profits.*

You may recall the 3 ways to grow your business that I discussed earlier:

1) You gain more customers.
2) You get your existing customers to spend more money with you.
3) You get your existing customers to purchase more frequently.

Immediately after the sale is one of the best ways to get them to do #2...spend more money with you.

Why? They're already favorable to you and/or your company. They've got their credit card out. And they have money to spend. And most importantly, they are a proven buyer in your niche market. Now is the perfect time to sell them again.

I know it seems at odds with common sense. Most people don't want to upset their new customers. They're afraid they'll want an immediate refund. They're afraid of alienating them, pissing them off.

Look, nothing could be farther from the truth...UNLESS you give them an offer they're not interested in.

An example I like to give is if they order a product from you that tells them how to grow bigger and more delicious peppers, then you try to sell them a product that tells them how to grow bigger watermelons, it may bomb. They're interested in *peppers*, not watermelons.

Yes, some of them might be interested in general gardening, and growing fruits and vegetables, but you want to be a specific as possible. You want to target them and match your offer to their needs and wants and desires as closely as possible.

Maybe they'd be more interested in *recipes* that include their homegrown peppers. You'll likely have to test and/or do some research to see what they want, but believe me, it'll pay off handsomely in the end.

There's another reason why including a follow-up offer in the welcome email is a good idea. **It's the one email you KNOW they will read!**

The Six Figure Sales Funnel
ANTICIPATING THEIR NEEDS AND REDUCING SUPPORT TICKETS

Obviously your welcome email will contain a link to the download page or membership site, if applicable. You'll also want to give them the support link. I also talked about including a relevant follow-up offer.

There's something else it should contain, too. A list of frequently asked questions (FAQs) and their answers (or a link to one on your site).

Being new customers, they may have questions. This is where getting good feedback really helps, which I'll talk about in a moment. You obviously want to anticipate their questions up front and answer them.

This works in your favor by reducing support requests, but it also works in your customer's favor, too. Do you think they'd rather have to log a support ticket and wait for an answer, or would they rather have the answer at their fingertips?

I know which one I'd prefer, and it's little things like that which make a difference in the relationship you build with them. Who knows! One of those customers may appreciate the ease of doing business with you and become one of your best "A" list customers!

THE IMPORTANCE OF TESTIMONIALS AND FEEDBACK

In addition to having your customers spend more money with you, you'll undoubtedly want testimonials, case studies, and specific feedback.

The importance of testimonials and case studies are obvious. You can add them to your sales letter, website, emails, and other marketing materials to boost your credibility, which will ultimately lead to more sales.

But never underestimate the importance of feedback. And by feedback, I don't just mean generalizations about how easy the ordering process was or their satisfaction. Those are important things, but what you're *really* after is the golden nuggets, the types of products they'd be interested in, market testing and that sort of thing.

And don't forget to ask them about the ease of use of your product, the ordering process, product fulfillment, everything. For every one person who tells you about an issue or pet peeve, there are probably 10 or more that are thinking it, but *don't* tell you. You have an opportunity to address each concern, or at a minimum explain it in your FAQ section, which you'll send them in the welcome email.

ASK THEM FOR REFERRALS AND MAKE IT WORTH THEIR WHILE

You're probably familiar with "tell-a-friend" scripts. If not, these basically handle the mechanics of giving your customers and prospects an "ethical bribe" for referring other people to your website, where you have the chance to sell them or have them join your list.

I've tested them and have had some mixed results. They DO work, but unfortunately a lot of the emails those scripts generate get caught in the recipients' spam filters.

You'll have to make up your own mind by testing them yourself and seeing how they work. In some non-IM niches they do exceedingly well. But unfortunately they are looked at increasingly as spam these days.

The working *concept* of those scripts, however, are as true today as they ever were. The key is to reward the referrer AND the person he is referring.

Dan Kennedy talks about a brilliant and proven way to do this in one of his many marketing books. The technique involves sending your customers a letter with 2 gift certificates: one for them to use, and one for them to pass along to a friend (or even better, 2 for them to pass along to 2 of their friends).

It's usually the case that when you give someone a gift certificate of a certain size (which is different for every product and industry...you'll need to test to determine your own "sweet spot"), they'll spend more than the amount of the gift.

There are all kinds of ways you can use this for holiday and other promotions, but the concept is the same: you reward your customers *and* the people they refer.

Leave this technique out of your email sequence, and you're missing out on an unrealized profit center for you.

EXCEED THEIR EXPECTATIONS WITH UNANNOUNCED BONUSES

Everybody loves to receive a gift they didn't anticipate. Unannounced bonuses after they've bought gives them even greater value and demonstrates your willingness to over deliver on your promises.

It adds customer loyalty and reduces refund rates. And it increases the likelihood they'll refer others to you, as well as recommend and endorse you.

The "bonuses" can even be in the form of additional content to help them with product consumption. For example, a video showing them how to do a certain task or get a desired result by using your product.

There's not much else to be said on that topic except for a couple guidelines:

The Six Figure Sales Funnel

1. **Make sure the bonus is relevant to the product they've purchased.** Just like back-end sales, you don't want to bombard them with stuff they don't want or need, even if it *is* free. The best bonuses are ones that allow them to get even MORE value out of the product they purchased from you.

2. **Your bonus should stand on its own as a product.** It should contain real value, and be something you could sell outright. Giving them junk won't fool them into thinking you're giving them "something extra." If anything, it'll make them think twice about you and your product. **In some cases, crap bonuses can actually reduce the perceived value in the product they paid for and <u>increase refunds</u>.**

3. **The timing of when you give extra bonuses should be tested or at least well-reasoned.** For example, do you think it's better to give them valuable bonuses they don't expect before or after you ask them for a referral? (Answer: Both, but give your better bonus first!)

CONSTRUCTING YOUR AUTORESPONDER SEQUENCES

> *"No matter what your product is, you are ultimately in the education business. Your customers need to be constantly educated about the many advantages of doing business with you, trained to use your products more effectively, and taught how to make never-ending improvement in their lives."*
> —Robert G Allen

PREMADE AUTORESPONDER SEQUENCES: BEYOND THE MOUTH OF THE SALES FUNNEL

Once a person has responded to your lead generation system and given you their contact information they have now entered into your sales funnel. They have gone from "suspect" to "prospect" and Step 1 of the sales funnel, as I described previously, is complete. Now your immediate goal is to progress to Step 2 where you convert the individual from a non-paying lead into a paying customer.

The timing of your contact with the person at this stage is crucial as their receptivity to you is often at its highest while you are at the forefront of their mind, having just provided them with something of outstanding value. In a nutshell, you are in the person's good books right now so you want to do everything you can to take advantage of that fact.

This is where premade autoresponder sequences come into play. You can't afford to miss the opportunity to reach a person when they are open to your offers. As you build the number of contacts you have the only way you can possibly reach all of them at these crucial moments is through automation. A well crafted series of emails scheduled to automatically go out at set intervals can take your prospect from the mouth of the sales funnel right through to becoming an "A" customer with little to no direct involvement from you.

I recommend creating three sequences of emails before you even let out a whisper about any given product: a pre-sales sequence, a post-sales sequence and a pre-launch sequence. Having these autoresponders poised and ready to go the moment you announce your product will let you strike while the iron is hot. From then on they will automate the process of making well timed contacts that will continue to guide your prospects and customers further into your sales funnel.

KEYS TO AUTORESPONDER SUCCESS

There are a few key points that you should consider when creating each of the emails in your autoresponder sequences.

Getting your emails opened

I mentioned earlier that getting your email opened depends on the subject line and the sender's name. Keep all your emails coming from the same name so people get familiar with you. Try to create subject lines that attract attention, but always make sure they are relevant to the body of your email. Even if you get someone to open your email but then make them feel like they were "suckered" into it, you'll lose their attention and most likely their trust right away.

Personalization

Most mailing list managers give you the option of including the name of the recipient in the email by inserting a placeholder such as [[firstname]]. This allows you to use the person's name in the subject line and in the email itself. For example:

The Six Figure Sales Funnel

```
Subject: [[firstname]], Here are your
downloads.
Body: Hi [[firstname]],
```

I don't include the person's name in the subject of every email I send out as sometimes it can flag the message as spam. Also, it keeps things fresh to mix up the subject line format a little as you move through your autoresponder sequences. An additional tip is to avoid capitalizing every word in the subject as though it were the title of a magazine article. If you only capitalize the person's name and the first word of the subject line it makes the email appear more as though it is coming from a friend. Wherever you can, make your emails seem warm and conversational rather than cold and formal.

Calls to action

Every email has a purpose and while sometimes all that will be is to provide valuable content and build a relationship, it will usually be to get the reader to take a specific action. The vast majority of the time you should choose only one thing per email that you want the reader to do so that you don't distract or confuse them with multiple calls to action. The call to action should be placed multiple times throughout the email. For example, if you want a person to visit a particular website, place the link towards the beginning, at the end and through the body of the email.

The Six Figure Sales Funnel

There are certain emails where you will include other calls to action and allow "link leakage" but this should only occur when you are trying to provide highly valuable content to earn trust early in the sequence. In these kinds of pure content or soft selling emails you should still place your main call to action throughout the content.

Pure content, soft selling & hard selling

In a nutshell there are three kinds of emails you will create for your autoresponder sequences. Pure content emails, soft sell emails and hard sell emails.

Pure content emails are designed to build trust and credibility with your prospect/customer and will include little to no promotion of your own products. In these emails the goal is to provide information and tips that are as helpful to the reader as possible while mentioning your own products in passing or sometimes not at all.

Soft sell emails will also primarily focus on information and tips designed to assist the reader but at the same time they will educate on the key selling points of your product. For example, you might explain a particular concept, describe how that concept can be used to benefit the reader, and then lead into how your product can help bring about that benefit. You might also include a call to action that takes the reader to a location where you apply more soft sell tactics, such as an educational video with a brief mention of your product at the end.

Hard sell emails are where the major focus of the email is describing the specific benefits of your product. You may still seek to educate the reader but the main thrust of the email is to directly communicate the major selling points of your product. Your call to action in a hard sell email is always either a link to your sales letter or in some cases a checkout link to purchase your product.

Your goal should be to mix up these three kinds of email throughout your sequence. Typically the soft sell email forms the majority of your sequence with the pure content and hard sell emails in the minority. Also, you will usually place your pure content towards the start of your sequence to build trust, and your hard sell emails towards the end when you have built a relationship with the reader. Some emails won't fall strictly into one category but will instead be halfway in between two, so you can gradually turn the dial from pure content to hard sell as you move through the sequence.

Split testing

Split test every email you write so that you can tweak the content for optimum click through rate. There's no need to gamble with guesswork on what should be included in your copy. Test everything and tweak until you feel you have the best possible versions of each of your emails. Split testing is a particularly useful technique to apply if you can enlist the help of a copywriter more experienced than yourself to give feedback on your emails. You can apply the feedback they give you and find out exactly what changes are working for you.

THE PRE-SALES SEQUENCE: WHERE LEADS BECOME CUSTOMERS

The purpose of the pre-sales sequence is to take a brand new lead by the hand and walk them down the path to becoming a paying customer. Due to the fact that your lead will have signed on to access an incentive you have offered the very first email in this sequence will always be the same; a message thanking the person for subscribing and an immediate presentation of the download link. After you provide the download link you can move into preselling your actual product.

The way to do this is by first providing information on the benefits of the incentive itself and then moving seamlessly into touching on some of the key selling points of your product. The key here is to be subtle. You know that the person is interested in the incentive they signed up for so keep the focus mainly on the benefits it offers and tie in some of the relevant benefits of your product. You'll have an entire autoresponder sequence behind this email so you don't need to rush the process and risk diminishing the trust the lead currently has for you.

The emails that follow in the sequence should each cover different aspects or concepts behind your main product. You can run through your sales letter and pull out the key points then expand on them in individual emails. As mentioned previously you can mix things up by using a combination of soft selling, hard selling and pure content designed to educate the reader. You'll find that a mixture like this will be more effective than just sending hard sells out every time and that people are more willing to stay subscribed to your list.

In the body of your emails aim to be warm and conversational and don't be afraid to repeat key points as this will give you a better chance of catching skim readers. You should also plan to include an email with case study results relevant to your product and one that presents testimonials and feedback that you've received.

Summary: Example Pre-Sales Sequence

The following is an example sequence that you can use to base your own autoresponder plan on. Remember though that every market is different so consider your own audience and your specific offer, and split test the emails and sequence that you use.

1. Thankyou/welcome. Call to action: download what they registered for. Pure content email, educate about the download. Send immediately.

The Six Figure Sales Funnel

2. Tip with promotion in P.S. Pure content/soft sell email. Send after 1 day.
3. Tip with promotion in P.S. Soft sell email. Send after 2 days.
4. Tip with promotion in P.S. Soft sell email. Send after 4 days.
5. Tip with case studies that relate to product. Soft sell with small hard sell aspects. Send after 6 days.
6. Tips with more direct reference to product. Soft to hard sell email. Send after 7 days.
7. Testimonials and social proof. Hard sell with main focus on others' opinions. Send after 10 days.
8. Tip with promotion in P.S. Soft sell email. Send after 14 days.
9. Tip with promotion in P.S. Soft sell with small hard sell aspects. Send after 16 days.
10. Tips with more direct reference to product. Soft to hard sell email. Send after 18 days.
11. Last chance email, last in the series. Hard sell. Send after 21 days.

THE POST-SALES SEQUENCE: BUILDING RELATIONSHIPS, BUILDING PROFITS

The Six Figure Sales Funnel

The post-sales sequence kicks into action immediately after you have converted a lead into a paying customer. Your goal in this sequence is to move your customer further along the sales funnel, to gain additional customers via referral, and to get feedback on your product.

In order to get your customer moving towards the desired "A" grade status you will need to make them feel like you have over delivered on your offer. Build your relationship with them and establish their trust and loyalty to you. You want to stay present in the mind of the customer in a positive way. The following is a five part suggested sequence you can use to accelerate this process.

Email 1: Thankyou / Welcome

As soon as a person makes a purchase you should send them an email thanking them or welcoming them to your service. Let them know that you appreciate their business. This is also the point where you can anticipate the customer's needs and address them before they ever ask you for assistance. Have an FAQ page prepared for your product and include a link to it in this initial email. You can also link to any other key information pages such as training videos or a help desk. Being proactive with this information lets the customer know you are there to support them.

As mentioned earlier, this is also an excellent time to make them an upsell offer. They have already shown that they are interested in your products and are willing to spend their money with you. Include a promotion in the P.S. to a **relevant** offer that will compliment the product they just purchased from you.

Email 2: Follow up

This email should be sent a couple of days after the thank you email to touch base with the customer and again remind them you are there to provide support. Include the links to key pages like the FAQ once again. You might also like to point them to additional training material now that they have had some time to orient themselves with the product. You should not plan to include any specific promotion in this email but if you do be sure to refer the customer to additional training material. You have the option to add a soft sell to the training material itself.

Email 3: Testimonial & feedback request

After the customer has owned the product for around five days it is the perfect time to send out a brief questionnaire asking for feedback on the product. This questionnaire gives you the chance to collect testimonials as well as information to help you improve the product.

Ask for their opinion on what they liked most about the product and what they would like to see improved upon. The answers to these questions can not only lead to favorable comments that can be added to your sales copy, but will also potentially help you adapt your product into something that even more people will buy.

You can also ask questions that will tip you off as to what kind of products the customer might potentially purchase in the future. A simple way to frame this kind of question is to offer a list of items and ask the person to rank those items from 1 to 5 in the order they have the greatest interest in.

At the end of the questionnaire ask for permission to use their comments as testimonials. Advise that prior to using any of the person's comments you will contact them and confirm the exact wording with them. Also, give the customer an incentive to return this questionnaire to you by letting them know you will place the address to their (non affiliate) website under any testimonial they offer.

Email 4: Help & backend offers

In this email you can point customers to specific elements of the product and expand on or remind them of why this element is important. You can describe the benefits that this aspect of the product provides and then tie in a promotion of a **related** backend offer. At this point you should have built enough good will from the relationship building you have done so far and the person's satisfaction with your product to see good results from the upsell.

Email 5: Unannounced bonus

In this email you should check in with the customer again and tell them you hope they have been exploring and trying out the product. Here is where you get the chance to exceed the customer's expectations by giving them a free bonus that they had no idea was coming. This bonus should be of outstanding quality and something you would expect to charge good money for as a standalone item. This is one of the most effective things you can do to keep the relationship and the trust building with the customer and let them know you're there to support them.

Summary: The Post-Sales Sequence

1. Thankyou/welcome. Pure content / soft sell email. Send immediately
2. Follow up. Pure content email. Send after 2 days
3. Testimonial & feedback request. Pure content email. Send after 5 days
4. Help & backend offer. Soft sell email. Send after 9 days
5. Unannounced bonus. Pure content email. Send after 14 days

THE PRE-LAUNCH SEQUENCE: START WITH A BANG!

The pre-launch sequence is very much like the pre-sales sequence and in some parts can be virtually identical. The key difference here is that given you are running this sequence prior to launch you won't be able to include a link to your sales letter until the very end. The other difference is that because you have no product to sell at the start of the sequence you can instead include relevant affiliate offerings where you feel it is appropriate.

You should remember that your goal with this sequence is to "sell the mystery" and build anticipation for the release of your product. Try not to give away too much information at once so that your content becomes a tease that leaves the reader curious to find out more.

You can build the mystery around the product by also asking the reader to keep the contents of your emails to themselves. Ironically, this request for secrecy can actually afford you the opportunity to have **more** word of mouth spread. You can include a link to a "tell a friend" page, as I described earlier, and suggest to the reader that if they do want to tell someone about this upcoming product they can follow the link and fill in their friend's information. To encourage the person to refer a friend you should offer them a bonus for doing so. You can then sell the benefits of the bonus itself and place the link to the "tell a friend" page throughout your description of the bonus.

As you move through the pre-launch sequence most of your emails can be the same as your pre-sales emails, with your testimonials email (if you have one prior to launch) going out second last. Around half way through the sequence you can also give away a small sample of your product to get subscribers a taste of what they will be getting. The final email should go out on the actual day of the product launch. This is the equivalent of the final email in the pre-sales sequence and is your big push to get people through the doors and buying the product.

Summary: Suggested Pre-Launch Sequence

1. Thankyou / welcome. Pure content. Send immediately. Get the reader interested with some solid helpful content. Potentially include an affiliate offer in the P.S.

2. What is the product & tell a friend. Soft sell email. Send after 2 days. Start to "sell the mystery". Offer a bonus to tell a friend.

The Six Figure Sales Funnel

3. Matches pre-sales email number 2. Pure content/soft sell email. Send after 3 days. Give a free sample of part of your product.

4. Matches pre-sales email number 4. Soft sell email. Send after 6 days.

5. Matches pre-sales email number 6. Soft to hard sell email. Send after 10 days

6. Testimonial email. Hard sell with main focus on others' opinions. Matches pre-sales email number 7. Send after 12 days

7. Launch notification. Hard sell email. Send after 15 days

INSTANT OPT-IN SURGE: HOW TO GET QUALIFIED LEADS SUBSCRIBING TO YOUR LIST IN RECORD NUMBERS

INTRODUCTION

There are as many ways to drive traffic to your website as there are trees in the forest. Now, qualified traffic, well that's a different story. You don't want to spend good money or time getting petrified wood collectors to your fly fishing site. You want diehard fly fishers to come, eager to read your content and subscribe to your list.

But even getting highly qualified visitors to your site doesn't have to be time-consuming or cost a fortune. It all depends on how you *leverage* your resources. Your articles. Your blog posts. Your posts on discussion forums. Cheap or free ways to get offline traffic to your site, too.

In fact, in this very special book, I discuss some of my favorite ways to get interested visitors to my sites, where they opt in to my lists and subscribe to my ezines and mini-courses. I'll also share some of my secrets to getting those visitors to opt in to your list once they arrive at your site.

Of course the ultimate goal is to make a profit. But before that happens, you need to develop a relationship with your prospects. You want to get to know them. And you want them to get to know you and what you have to offer.

This isn't a book about the importance of building your list. I'm assuming you already know what a highly responsive list means to you and your business.

Rather, these methods are the ones that cost me the least and deliver the best results. I've built several lists from scratch using nearly all of these methods in some form or another. The ones I haven't tried yet were passed along to me by friends and colleagues, who *have* used them to build their lists and churn some nice tidy profits.

The four primary methods I use and recommend are: writing and syndicating articles, leveraging discussion forum posts, joint ventures, and offline marketing. They have proven their worth to me many times over, and I highly recommend you at least try them.

In fact, no matter how many things you've tried in the past, and no matter how successful you are today, I can't see you walking away without getting at least one or two new gems to test from this concise, but meaty section.

So with that, let's get started with one of the best ways to get responsive visitors to your website: writing and publishing articles.

WRITING AND PUBLISHING ARTICLES

It's fairly well-know that one of the better ways for building a list or generating website traffic is by writing articles. But just as important as writing the articles is where they are distributed and used. How they are promoted. You're going to find that that's going to be the key to getting traffic to your site and building your list. Articles can be submitted to directories, posted on your blog, on your website, on forums, wherever you have an opportunity to reach people that may be interested in your niche.

So you want your articles to be as distributed as widely as possible all over the Internet and in the offline world wherever possible. For example, here some sites where you can submit your articles, and where other newsletter authors and publishers will come to get content for other publications:

- http://www.articledashboard.com
- http://www.articlealley.com
- http://www.goarticles.com
- http://www.articlecity.com
- http://ezinearticles.com
- http://www.ideamarketers.com
- http://www.marketing-seek.com

By letting others publish your articles in their ezines, your website can gain even greater exposure. Nothing terribly new about that.

Where most people fail is how they attempt to get readers of their articles to take action. That is, getting them to both:

1) Visit your website

and…

2) Get them to opt in to your list

It takes some planning and work on your part to make this desired result happen.

- ✓ Writing your article takes time and effort.
- ✓ Getting someone to publish your article in their ezine takes more effort.

✓ Getting people to read your published article takes even more effort.

✓ It takes additional effort to get people to visit your website after reading the article.

✓ And finally, it takes effort on top of that to get your website visitors to opt in to your list.

Is it any wonder most people aren't as successful as they could be? There are many places along the way for missed opportunities, where potential subscribers will slip through the cracks.

Not only that, but you're competing with tons of other marketers who are trying to do the same thing. The odds are definitely stacked against you.

But in this section, I'll show you some techniques to significantly improve your odds, techniques that 95 percent of all article authors aren't using. Do you think this will give you an edge? It will...if you *use* these techniques and actually put them to the test.

First, let me talk about some of the basics of writing your article. If you go to article directories, you'll find that too many of the articles you see there don't even incorporate these basic response-boosting tactics.

The title of your article is key, so choose it wisely. Your article title is your headline for your article. And in a sales letter, the purpose of your headline is to get your letter read, right? Well, in this case, the purpose of your title is to get your article read. You'll find that many of the same principles of writing headlines apply to choosing your title. *You want people to stop what they're doing and read your article right then and there.*

That means titles that are benefit-driven will outperform those that aren't. Your readers want to know what's in it for them. So you need to craft your title accordingly. This is no time to be vague or clever.

And before you choose your title, you'll need to know a bit about your target audience. Their wants, desires, needs. Their problems. What's on their minds. In short, you need to fit the message of the article, and your title in particular, to what your target market wants. And by target market, I mean those who you ultimately want to come to your website and opt in to your list. So the more targeted the message, the better.

Your title should…

- ✓ Address something desirable
- ✓ Be as specific as possible
- ✓ Convey a sense of urgency
- ✓ Make a promise
- ✓ Be intriguing

The more of these points you include in your title, the better you can generally expect your readership to be.

The Six Figure Sales Funnel

Here are some examples:

The Top X Ways To _____

The Top 5 Ways To Lose 5 Pounds in a Week
The Top 10 Ways To Knock 5 Strokes Off Your Next
Round of Golf

How To _____ In _____

How To Double Your Profits In 30 Days
How To Get Out of Debt In 3 Simple Steps

How To _____…Even If _____

How To Make the Lottery Pay Off…Even If You
Never Invest a Dime
How To Turn Your Hobbies Into Cash…Even If
You've Never Sold Anything

The Quick and Easy Formula for _____

The Quick and Easy Formula for Finding That Special
Someone
The Quick and Easy Formula for Selling Your Home

____ Little Known Tips for _____

The Six Figure Sales Funnel

7 Little Known Tips for Training Your Labrador

3 Little Known Tips for Roughing It in the Wilderness

The _____ Hidden Costs of _____

The 10 Hidden Costs of Buying Your New Home

The Sneaky Hidden Costs of Renting a Car on Your Next Vacation

_____: The Proven _____

Direct Mail: The Proven Way to Reactivate Former Customers

A.I.D.A.: The Proven Formula For Sales Conversions

One final word about titles: Remember that when someone is browsing an article directory, they are seeing your article title alongside tons of others. It's kind of like the Yellow Pages. The Yellow Pages are one of the most competitive places to advertise. Why? Because your prospects see your ads right alongside your competitors'. You definitely NEED to stand out from the clutter. Your title should be about your prospect's needs, wants, and desires. *It should be about the person reading the article, not the article itself.*

This becomes even more critical when a publisher looking for content is browsing an article directory. After all, which do you think will bring you more exposure: a reader browsing articles or a publisher with a 100,000-person subscriber list who publishes *your* article?

Your first paragraph will keep them reading—or not. After your title, your opening paragraph guides them into the main body of your article, so you'll want it to be interesting, and an extension of your title. Some good ways to keep that interest going are to:

- ✓ Present a problem
- ✓ Set the stage with a story, anecdote, or quote
- ✓ Ask a question
- ✓ Reveal an interesting or startling fact
- ✓ Present an overview
- ✓ Paint an emotional picture

Use proven formulas. Just like a sales letter, proven formulas boost readership and response in articles too.

- ✓ **Problem-Agitate-Solution** – You present a problem, then agitate it further. Finally the solution is hinted at towards the end of the article (with an incentive for them to go to your website to get the full picture).

- ✓ **Before and After** – I was fat, now I'm thin. I was poor, now I'm rich. I was a hack, now I'm a scratch golfer.

✓ **Useful, but Incomplete** – Give just enough information to entice them, but leave them wanting more (which your website will provide).

✓ **Frequently asked questions** – Include some great ones, but leave some out to be placed on your website. Be sure to let them know in your resource box at the end of the article that there are more at your site.

✓ **Share a specific set of points.**
   o 5 Steps to Making a Fortune on eBay
   o How to Speed Up Your Metabolism in 3 Easy Steps
   o 10 Ways to Write Better Ads
   o 3 Keys to a Greener Lawn
   o 7 Quick Tips for Self-Defense

Position yourself as the expert, but don't be condescending. This is a given, but it's worth mentioning. Yes, you want to be seen as an authority on the subject, but you don't want to come across as arrogant or a "know-it-all." Remember these are real people reading your article. If you offend them, you've lost them. Of course the same can be said for off-color or offensive remarks. When in doubt, leave it out.

Your resource box should present itself as the next logical step. The article should transition nicely right into the resource box. You want them to go to your website, so your resource box should hint at more information to be found on the topic.

Give them an "ethical bribe." Your resource box should also give a no-brainer offer. An "ethical bribe" designed to entice them. Just like you need a premium to get them to opt in to your list, you also need a premium of sorts to get them to your website in the first place.

Leverage your article wherever possible. In short, you want that article reused as much as possible all over the Internet (and offline as well).

✓ Post it in the article directories.

✓ Post it on all relevant forums.

✓ Submit it to search engines.

✓ Post it on your blog.

✓ Post it on your website.

✓ Encourage others to publish it in their ezines.

✓ Include your article in viral ebooks to be passed around the web.

✓ Offer your article as a premium report for other people's products. Expand on the article, if necessary, to make it a content-packed report.

✓ Offer it for others to use on their content sites (e.g. Adwords), membership sites, as part of a mini-course, anywhere your target market will be exposed to it.

✓ Offer it to your affiliates.

Give your best tip at the end of the article and your second best tip at the start – In a sales letter, we'd usually start off with our strongest benefit or point and work our way down to the lesser benefits from there. In an article, you often want that big bang at the end, just before they're led to your resource box. Also your last tip can carry the greatest weight if you lead up to it, by making all other tips depending on the final one, and by foreshadowing the final tip to come.

Then your resource box should offer something related to your final point. All they have to do is head over to your website.

Design your resource box like you would a headline – Similar to the effort you must put into your article title and the headline on your squeeze page, your resource box needs to contain a sense of urgency. It must tap anticipation, desire, curiosity, and/or other emotional hot buttons. <u>It must have a call to action</u>. And like your title, where the goal is to have your article read, the goal with your resource box is to get them to go to your website. Now, not tomorrow or next week.

And much like there should be congruency between a Google Adwords ad and the landing page headline, so must your resource box and headline on your squeeze page match. Think about it. If your resource box looked like the following:

About the Author

Jane Doe is a certified massage therapist, author, speaker and consultant. Watch her conduct her stress reduction workshop each month on video. Jane is giving free access to this private site, but only while charter memberships last. Join today at http://JaneDoeMassage.com.

...your headline your squeeze page should tie into that offer. Maybe:

"Jump to the Head of the Line and Get FREE Access To Jane Doe's Private Membership Forum...Before All Charter Memberships are Gone"

Or something like that. I just made that up, but you get the idea. Here's another example of a resource box with a good call to action:

John Smith is the author of the free 36-page report, "How to Turn Your Hobby into Your Own Personal ATM Machine." Head over to http://www.whatever.com for your free copy while supplies last.

Remember, everything in your article is designed to get them to go to your site. And everything at your site is designed to get them to subscribe to your list. So you really need two calls to action here—two incentives: one to get them to go to your website, and another one to get them to subscribe.

Let's look at another great way to get qualified traffic to your squeeze page: posting to forums.

POSTING TO FORUMS

Posting to discussions is a very fast and powerful way you can start expanding your list of subscribers in as little as *5 minutes*.

You can find forums about your niche very easily. Just Google the following:

+"your niche" +forum

or

+"your niche" +discussion board

Just be sure to check the posting guidelines for each forum before you post. The techniques I'm presenting here are generally acceptable on most forums, but you need to know what's allowed and what's not, especially when it comes to solicitations.

Here are some quick and easy ways to get pre-qualified traffic flowing your way:

Ask for suggestions or advice. Let's say you've written an article on your site entitled "15 Ways to Put the Romance Back in a Relationship." You could make a post asking folks to check out the article and see if you missed anything. Or you can ask for additional points to add to your article. Of course you'll have your opt in box at the end of the article with a compelling offer.

Let's say you've written an article on losing weight quickly. You could post a message like this: "If you had to lose 5 pounds in 2 weeks for a wedding, how would you do it?"

It's a great way to get both input and exposure for your article. You may also get other publishers who are interesting in your content for their ezines, leveraging that content even more.

Ask for a critique. If you don't mind getting honest feedback, many people will end up subscribing to your list. It's a more indirect and acceptable way to ask people to check out your site without blatant advertising. Plus, the feedback they give you may help to make your squeeze page even more compelling. Ask them if it would persuade them to give it a try, assuming they were in your target market (of course you already know they are by the forum you selected). And if they say no, ask them why. You can get valuable information on what they want (and don't want) this way.

There are two types of forums where you should ask for critiques: the niche forum itself and a marketing forum. You'll likely get more sign-ups from the niche forum, and good advice to test out from the marketing forum (although you'll get some opt ins there as well).

Ask your market what they want. It's one of the best ways to develop products and services they'll buy *and* give you ideas for articles, autoresponder content, your blog posts, whatever you need.

The way you would use this technique to get them to subscribe is to post something like, "what's your biggest question about building a web page?" Or "what's the single most important thing you'd like to know about brewing your own beer?"

The Six Figure Sales Funnel

Let them know you've already answered 7 questions (your 7 step mini-course loaded in your autoresponder), for example. Then they'll be more likely to sign-up. Make sure you point out that you'll add to your mini-course with the answers to the questions they've provided, and that they'll get answers to the existing questions in your mini-course PLUS the new ones when they subscribe. Everybody wins!

Offer a checklist or video tutorial. If someone asks how to research a niche market, give them a checklist of steps they can take. Or make a Camtasia tutorial video showing them how. Now that you've got them to your site, you'll want to "make them an offer they can't refuse."

Offer a list of resources. In addition to checklists, resource lists with website URLs make a great site for them to bookmark! Make sure you supply more than just links. Make it a huge info-page of information. A collection of resources, links to everything you have—articles, video, audio, your blog, other useful sites, tools, you name it.

This technique tends to work best when you set up a separate domain for the site. Make it a portal. You want people to come back again and again, so keep it fresh with content and up to date.

Solve a problem or give some help. If someone asks for help or asks a question, offer your experience and try to help them. But to maximize your odds of getting both the asker of the question and everyone else who reads the post to subscribe to your list, try to phrase your answer in one of the following two ways:

1) Give them tips, techniques, shortcuts, secrets, anything that offers both promise of exclusive information *and* fast results. A shortcut to success.

2) Whenever possible, supply them with specific results. Think about it. When you want to learn how to bowl a perfect game, you go to someone who has *bowled a perfect game*. When you want to know how to sing with a perfect pitch, you seek out someone who's already mastered that skill. If you want to lose 10 pounds, it carries more weight (no pun intended) if they person guiding you has *actually lost 10 pounds*. Do you see where I'm going with this?

And by helping them, maybe—just maybe—they'll click on he link in your signature to check out your website. If you direct them to a blog post or article you wrote to answer their question, they'll be even more likely to investigate.

The Six Figure Sales Funnel

In fact, here's a sneaky but completely ethical way to virtually guarantee you get an onslaught of new subscribers:

Find a hot topic. In most forums you should be able to determine how many times a forum had been read and/or how many posts it contains. You want to find one that's on fire. If it involves a highly emotional or controversial subject, so much the better, as these tend to grow very quickly and get read often.

Write an article about the subject being discussed. You know the topic is of interest to them or it wouldn't be so hot. In short, you are entering the conversation already in their minds. Your article will be current to the discussion, relevant to what's being discussed, and highly desired due to the hot nature of the topic. Your article should offer a solution if a problem is being discussed, a tutorial, a case study, a list of tips or shortcuts, whatever this audience is looking for (they're telling you right there in their posts).

If the forum allows it (most do), give it a compelling subject line when you post. What I mean is don't accept the default original subject already being passed from post to post within that thread. You want your subject to be intriguing and compelling, just like your headlines and article titles, but you may want to hint at being controversial as well. If it's a hotly discussed topic, people will read your post if they think it's "gonna be good." Above all, don't be boring.

Here are some quick examples on how you could begin your title with a "controversial edge:"

- I don't think so...
- I think you have it backwards...
- This is the best one I've seen...
- Umm...no...
- What I did was...
- That's good, but this is easier...
- Wait a minute...
- Why do that, when...
- Actually...
- Let me see if I got this straight...
- You can't go wrong with...
- What about....plus it's free!

4) Share a part of your article, and direct them back to your article for the rest, where you'll have an opt in box with a premium if they sign up. I suggest testing a mini-course or archive of articles relating to that topic if they subscribe (but call it something else).

Give them part of your article. Rather than posting your article in its entirety, give them the first part and redirect them to your blog or website to read the rest.

The Six Figure Sales Funnel

Obviously your title and lead must be strong, and you want to stop at a point that leaves them hanging.

Use an 800 Pound Gorilla and Search-Friendly Subjects. Here's a tip I picked up on Michel Fortin's forum. By posting your articles or content on "heavyweight" sites like Michel's, you'll get higher rankings in organic search engine searches. It's a no-brainer, but it's often not understood or used as well as it should.

Give 'em your best tip and leave them wanting more. Let's say you're browsing a blues guitar forum, and you see lot of discussion about learning to play guitar like Stevie Ray Vaughn. You put together a tutorial with tablature entitled, "*9 Stevie Ray Riffs You Can Learn to Play in an Hour.*" In your posted reply, you give them your best riff right there to show you've got the goods. Then send them to your tutorial for the other 8 riffs.

Or perhaps you're looking through a smoking cessation forum. Obviously these folks want to know the best ways to quit smoking. So after you write an article about it, you come back and announce "here are the exact steps I took to quit smoking…and I've been smoke-free for a year now." Remember, people would rather learn from someone who has already done it. If you can be that person, you'll have a steady stream of prospects following you back to your site wanting more. It just doesn't get any easier than this.

Include your list offer as a resource. When you find a hot discussion that lends itself well to a list of resources for that topic, by all means supply them with some. Just make sure YOU are included among those resources. For example, if you have a mini-course entitled, *"7 Ways to Stop Insomnia,"* you could write about *"Top 10 Free Insomnia Resources."* And of course you list your mini-course as one of the free resources.

And don't forget to leverage everything. Use your content for articles, blog posts, forum posts, a free PDF report, wherever you can.

Because your article contains FREE resources, it's likely that other ezine list owners will publish it. And as an extra incentive to get other list owners to publish it, you can allow them to add one of their own resources into your article. In fact, you can even offer the content with private label rights with the only condition being that your resource stays intact as is. That is, they can change anything else they want and even claim authorship, but your resource stays. And that means even more exposure for you.

JOINT VENTURES

Joint ventures (JVs) are one of the best ways to lure new leads and customers. By partnering with other businesses whose customers are part of your market, you have an additional profit center of incremental income. For example, an attorney can refer his clients to an accountant, and the accountant in turn refers clients to the attorney. It's a win/win situation, because many times a new business will need both an attorney and an accountant. Depending on which one they approach first (the lawyer or accountant), they'll be referred to the other.

JVs can go much further than this simple arrangement, however. They can be very complex, and there can be 3-way deals going on. The key to making these deals work is to make sure that you let a prospective JV partner know from the start that:

- You've discovered an additional profit center for them that they are probably unaware of (offer projected profits, if possible).

- The additional profit center will not detract in any way from their current income stream.

- The additional profit center will not incur any additional costs or labor on their part to implement.

- The additional profit center will not incur any risk whatsoever on their part.

- You will perform all of the leg work to set it up.

- They can stop at any time for any reason.

One Tip: If you try to set up a JV with a business, and they already have a deal in place with someone else, you can take that information to their competitor and say "Your biggest competitor is already doing this." And if your partner ever decides to stop the JV deal, you can go to their competitors and say the same thing (Hint: if you let them know you are going to do that, they may reconsider). Never feel that you have to partner with one specific business exclusively. Ideally you should have JV deals going on all over the place.

You can also do JVs between your business and another, or you can broker JVs between two different businesses and benefit in the middle.

FINDING JV PARTNERS

If you know of a company that sells a complementary but not competitive product or service as yours, you should subscribe to their list and watch their content sent to you over time. That will give you a feel for their marketing style and the types of affiliates/joint ventures they promote.

One way to find such potential alliance partners is via the good "old fashioned" search engines. Only in this case, you're going to drill down a bit deeper.

Google is one of the best search engines to use when locating JV partners, because of the tools available at your disposal when searching.

The trick is to know what to search for and to use Google's research tools correctly. Here are some of my favorite ways.

1) Use the *inurl* search.

You can go to Google and type in: *inurl:[keyword]* to find web addresses that contain your keyword in the full web address name itself (including parts that *aren't* part of the root domain name).

For example, typing *inurl:mortgage* might give me:

- http://http://www.mortgage.com
- http://www.mortgage-calc.com
- http://en.wikipedia.org/wiki/Mortgage
- http://hometown.aol.com/aaamortg/mortgage.html
- http://www.mortgage-express.co.uk

...and much more.

Note that they all contain the word "mortgage" in the domain name, subdomain name or a file or directory name within the domain.

2) Use the *allinurl* search.

Similar to the *inurl* search, the *allinurl* search allows you to type in *allinurl:[keyword phrase]* and return all addresses that contain that phrase in the domain name, subdomain name or a file or directory name within the domain.

For example, typing *allinurl:weight loss* might return:

- http://www.weight-loss-institute.com
- http://www.technorati.com/tags/weight+loss
- http://www.drugs.com/weight-loss.html
- http://weight-loss.one-pharmacy.com
- http://www.mayoclinic.com/health/weight-loss/WT99999

...for starters.

You'll be able to narrow your focus even more.

3) Use the *intitle:[keyword]* **and** *allintitle:[keyword phrase]*

Similar to *inurl* and *allinurl*, this search returns the keyword or keyword phrase in the title of the web page.

For example, *intitle:exercise* might return (the bolded text is my addition):

American Council On **Exercise**
(http://www.acefitness.org)

Exercise: A Healthy Habit to Start and Keep -- familydoctor.org
(http://familydoctor.org/059.xml)

MedlinePlus: **Exercise** and Physical Fitness
(http://www.nlm.nih.gov/medlineplus/exerciseandphy sicalfitness.html)

Notice the keyword *exercise* appears in each of the titles, but may or may not appear in the URLs.

And *allintitle:corporate law* might return:

Corporate Law - Guide to Corporate and Business Law
(http://www.hg.org/corp.html)

Delaware **Corporate Law** Clearinghouse - Chancery Court, Court of ...
(http://corporate-law.widener.edu)

Gulf **Law**: **Corporate** Laws in Arab Middle East, Company **Law** Guide ...
(http://gulf-law.com)

Company **law** databases and **corporate** regulatory issues in India
(http://www.companylawonline.com)

Look at the last two above. Notice how Google didn't only return web pages with the exact phrase "*corporate law*". It returned those that had ALL of the words in the phrase in its title, in any order.

If you want only the exact phrase returned, place double quotes around the keyword phrase, like this: *allintitle:"corporate law"*

Now let's look at some ways you can use both online and offline JVs to grow your list.

JV your list building: large list. If you have a large list, one of the easiest ways to build it even further is to do a cross mailing. That is, you partner with another large list owner in your target market. You send out his message to your list, he sends out your message to his list. Simple. Just remember, once your prospects or customers are on another list that sells to them, there is increased message clutter. That is, they are now being pitched by your JV partner AND you. It's a tradeoff you need to consider.

JV your list building: small list. Ok, if your existing list isn't large enough to warrant a cross JV mailing as described above, here's a clever way to build your list up quickly. I've done this, but not to the extent I should. I've got more deals like this in the works. Here's how it works:

Let's say your list is on the small side. "John Smith" has a huge list. You want to JV with him, but a cross swap isn't going to persuade him. You need to be the middleperson between John Smith and another large list owner.

"Jane Doe" is another huge list owner. What if you can put John Smith and Jane Doe together to do a cross mailing, and you get exposure as well. Instead of a cut of profits, you agree to get a slice of the list. In other words, perhaps in order to get onto Jane's list from John's, they have to come through you first. Or, you could have John mail his list with the agreement that whatever prospects Jane gets, she'll share with you. It's a win/win/win situation, because all of you are gaining new prospects on your lists.

John gets some of Jane's list.

Jane gets some of John's list.

You get some of Jane's list. Or, ideally, you get some of both lists. You are the dealmaker. It wouldn't have happened without you, so depending on the deal you make, why shouldn't you get access to both lists?

Another way to JV your list building: small list. Your list is your greatest asset, right? But if you only have 1,000 names where 50,000 or 100,000 is the norm (more is better, right?), then why not JV a list exchange. Bear with me. It's true that you may not have much to offer to the list owner of 100,000+ names, when you only have 1,000. But it can be done.

One way to do this? Ok, let's pretend that I convince a speaker to do a teleseminar with me that I know at least 2 or 3 other 100k+ list size owners would love to tell their subscribers about. Let's couple that with the fact that these list owners want to build their lists even more. And you do too. You could make a deal with some of these list owners that whoever opts in to your teleseminar, you'll do a solo mailing of a product of their choice to the entire list if they promote the call. Remember they're delivering a message to their list that their list would be interested in, and they're interested in getting the names of the other list owners that will opt-in. So you act as the middle-person and make all sides happy, while greatly adding to the size of your list.

I've personally done this, and I've got some big promotions on the way that will grow my list even further. All you need to do is to contact these people and let them know how they benefit from the arrangement.

Will everyone welcome the deal? No. But there are plenty who will. And everyone wins (those are the best kinds of deals, by the way). This is one of those ideas that will work just as good online as they do offline.

Seek out other businesses that cater to your market. I used the lawyer and accountant example in the introduction to this JV section. A realtor may JV with moving companies, custom framers, carpet cleaners, pest control services, lawn care companies, painters, electricians, plumbers, the list goes on. Just be sure to JV with those businesses who have products and/or services your customers may need (i.e. a realtor JVing with a video game company doesn't make much sense).

Make a list of businesses who want and need a constant flow of leads: lawyers, doctors, dentists, realtors, home remodeling services, carpet cleaners, pest control services, etc. Broker deals between them where there is a fit to generate leads.

JV mailings. For generating leads where it's not cost-effective, direct mail can be prohibitively expensive. That's why card decks and Value-Paks are so popular. But aside from those types of mailings, you can always partner with a non-competitor (or two or three) that offer a complementary or similar offer with the same target market as yours. By splitting the cost of the mailing, you still get your message out, but at a much-reduced cost.

JV inserts/flyers/circulars. Similar to JV mailings, you could arrange to have your flyer, insert, or circular inserted into another publication already being mailed. This "hitching a ride" approach works best when your audience is targeted, although newspaper inserts are popular with local bricks and mortar businesses. The JV part comes into play when you pay so much per lead or a percentage of all sales resulting from the arrangement. Depending on your price structure, you can pay a percentage of the first sale only, or a tiered approach where a smaller percentage is paid for all first year purchases, a percentage of the back-end purchase, etc. You need to determine what types of deals bring in the biggest profits for you, while still providing a valuable incentive for your JV partners. And that really goes for any type of deal.

Lead generation JVs. Find out what other businesses your target market visits. For example, I sell to entrepreneurs, and a lot of them frequent the UPS Store and other such places. Fedex/Kinkos and other "copy shops" are also ideal places where I live. Many of these places don't capture their customer's name, address, email address, etc. So I made an arrangement with them. I setup "take ones," where they can take a brochure for free, go online to my website, fax me, or mail me their contact info, then I send them a free report relevant to them. I give their contact info to the store I JV with (and I notify the prospects of this fact...it hasn't seem to hurt my leads significantly so far). For those businesses (a Staples store, being one of them) that are stubborn, I offer to give them the contact info I collect from all the stores I JV with in their area. Again, you need to include a disclaimer when doing that, but in my tests, the benefit has outweighed the losses.

In a discussion with copywriter Michel Fortin recently, he mentioned that you need to really provide an incentive for these businesses to promote you. So the "take one" box may not be enough by itself. True, they are getting the contact info of some of their customers (something they themselves should be gathering), but if they don't know enough to get that information in the first place, they may not be as anxious to promote your free report or premium.

Endorsements. There are people and businesses that have a great personal relationship with their customers and prospects. They may not necessarily know this fact.

In fact, a lot of them don't even realize the amount of pull they have with their audience. People who recommend certain stocks or trends, people who give great content and information to their subscribers, people who give investment advice, generally people who have a certain rapport with their subscribers. They are the ones you want to target. If their niche is non-marketing-related, so much the better in order to cut through this niche's clutter. I know someone who targeted golf enthusiasts for a marketing product, simply because of their test results. In any case, if you can JV with this sort of person who will endorse your product or service, you have a huge advantage. It's simply one of the best ways to print money on demand. Please don't overlook this technique.

These people may not even realize the relationship they have with their list. So you would be well advised to start with those folks.

Look all around you. There are more ways to line up joint ventures and strategic alliances than you can shake a stick at. You just need to develop an open mindset that will soak up opportunities like a sponge. Reading the newspaper, business trade journals, and other publications, both online and offline, can kick start ideas in your head when you least expect them. So think of the JV examples I've provided in this report as just the beginning.

OFFLINE MARKETING

Offline list building is usually referred to as generating leads, but the concept is the same. The fact is, you should be doing both online and offline marketing. And just like your online marketing, you test different strategies and keep doing what works and get rid of what doesn't work. Well, the same goes for offline marketing.

If you're not doing both, you are missing out on some serious profits. Even if you are making $10K, $50K, or $100K a month online, why wouldn't you want more?

Consider that in the 15 countries with the highest rate of Internet usage, only 18% have Internet access. That means over 80% of your market never has a chance to hear your message. And the actual percentage is even higher, since many people use the Internet for email only. Even in the US, which has by far the largest share of Internet users, 37% of the population is not online -- that's over 110 million people!

But...consider this: of that potential 18% that are online and you do have the potential to reach, they are offline the majority of the time, where they won't see your message.

The Six Figure Sales Funnel

In other words, your target market is still likely larger in the offline world. By not marketing to them where they "live," you are missing out on a very big slice of the pie.

Most offline marketing techniques are fairly straightforward, and can be done for very cheaply or even free. Here are some of my favorites.

Classified ads. This is something everyone should be testing in some form or another. It's great for lead generations. You should still have a strong benefit-driven headline and a clear call to action. Free reports work very well with classifieds. My local paper, the Hartford Courant even has an ongoing deal of 3 lines for 3 days – for free! Even adding more lines only ends up costing a few bucks. With a price like that, there's no reason anyone with a website should not be testing ways to draw traffic to the site with classifieds.

Postcards. Yes, postcards are a form of direct mail, but it warrants its own category. Postcards are cheaper to produce and mail than full-blown direct mail packages or sales letters, and they are great for generating leads. Like classified ads, a free report or free gift often works well here. Postcards are also a great way to stay in touch with your customers and prospects, and they also work well as part of a sequence of mailings. A good place to go for customized postcards is http://www.usps.com (the US Postal Service website), because the USPS has partnered with a company that will print and mail your postcards for you! Best of all, you only pay for the postage (i.e. FREE printing costs). Hint: be sure to include yourself on the mailing list so you can get your own mailing as well.

Flyers. Who says you can't hire a high school student to stuff mailboxes or stick 'em under windshields? Obviously if you are selling a high-priced financial course, it would be better to target the windshields of a fancy hotel than your local Wal-Mart. And I believe the US Postal Service also prints them for you like they do postcards if you want to mail them. Check out http://www.usps.com

Networking. Your local Chamber of Commerce, trade shows, seminars, and anywhere your prospects hang out are all good opportunities for networking. In many cases, the hotel bar the night before the seminar is the best opportunity for making contacts. It's usually more effective to try to capture contacts and leads than to try to close a sale on the spot, so get your elevator speech ready and have plenty of business cards on hand.

Card decks. These stacks of index cards are mailed to targeted audiences. Each deck can contain anywhere from 50 to 200 cards or so, each with an advertisement or coupon. They may also double as a business reply card on back. Since your ad is mixed in with tons of others, it's especially important to have a great headline and layout that will stand out from the clutter.

Card decks are inexpensive because all of the advertisers are sharing the cost of the mailing. They can cost as little as three cents a prospect for large mailings. Even for smaller mailings, they are generally cheap, which is good for testing.

Make sure you choose your audience wisely. Card decks are great for targeting a niche. Free reports or books work especially well here, because the person flipping through the cards will be attracted to the word "FREE." As always, make sure there is a clear call to action. Multiple methods of response usually work better than a single method. For example, they can drop the card in the mail, call a free recorded message, go to your website, etc. And you may have some options with remnant space, so always try to negotiate a lower price (how hard is it for them to stick another card in their mailing...their costs are incremental and their profit is high even on remnant rates).

A couple other tips: When you see repeat advertisers in a deck, you have a pretty good idea that the deck is working for that ad. If that ad also targets your niche market, it may be a good one to test in. Also, test with copy that you already know works.

Package inserts. If you're going to mail out a product or package to a customer anyway, always tuck a sales letter for another product in the package. It won't cost you any more, and when your customer receives that package, he or she will be pleased with the product (assuming your product isn't junk) and be more favorable towards another purchase from you. You can also joint venture with other companies that target your niche market and get them to include your insert when shipping their product.

Teleseminars. Basically a conference call, we've all probably been on many of them. Some have organized them and have been speakers. They can be pure content (i.e. no obvious pitches) for strengthening social proof and building up anticipation for a new product to be released in the future. They can be a mixture of content and pitch. You can even arrange a series of them as a tele-course and charge big money to attend (Marc Goldman and Jay Abraham did this with a six-month long series, one per month, on joint ventures and deal making).

Word of mouth / viral marketing. The key here is create something that people will want to share. Yes, the "tell a friend" scripts are good online. But surely there's something you can think of to really "wow" them. You want to make them say "Wait until Jane sees this!"

One of the keys to making this work (and any sort of lead generation device) is to know your customer's lifetime value. In other words, what does your average customer in this market (using the type of lead generation you are doing) bring me in profits over their entire lifetime? Let's say it's $25,000. And let's say your method of gathering leads converts 10% of leads into customers. Do you think it's wise to spend $100 per lead of that type in your efforts? Seems like a no-brainer to me.

Creative business cards. Besides using both sides of your business cards and putting a compelling benefits-oriented message on it, there are many other creative ways to put your business card to work for you. Of course, odd-shaped and "rolodex-styled" cards stick out from the crowd as well. One real estate agent in California hands an extra three bucks and a business card to the toll collector as he crosses the bridge into San Francisco. He tells the toll collector that he wants to pay for the driver behind him, and asks him to give the driver his business card. Nine out of ten times, the driver calls, at least to say thank you. He's sold several expensive homes that way as a result.

A good lead generation device is to offer a free report or other gift on the back of the card. Then just distribute them where your prospects live.

At my local Munson's Chocolates outlet, Sales Manager Jim Florence has his business card fully imprinted with the company logo, name, phone number, and email address made out of…you guessed it…CHOCOLATE! (best business card I've ever eaten). A relatively new technology now allows Munson's to "print" in edible ink everything from text, images, logos, and photographs. With their business cards, customers get to taste their USP. How many other businesses offer that experience?

Issue a press release. An oldie, but goodie. The trick is to make sure your press release is a newsworthy event. For example, starting a new newsletter is not necessarily a newsworthy event (but it might in certain niche markets for smaller publications). Issuing a press release about a large donation you are giving, complete with relevant background story might be newsworthy. It all depends on your target audience and the publication(s). Editors pick up press releases if they think there is news for their readers. They do not care about you or your company. Your press release must be framed that way. "What's in it for me" is very relevant here.

IMPROVING YOUR OPT-IN CONVERSIONS

First, a word about name-squeeze pages. Squeeze pages, or the sales copy you use to get people to opt in to your list, have often been regarded as something that's less important than the actual sales copy for a product being sold. Nothing could be farther from the truth. In fact, as research shows it takes between seven and thirteen messages on average before someone will ultimately make a purchase, that list is more important than ever to build value and develop a relationship with your subscribers.

With the way things have evolved online, these days you need to write longer and more persuasive copy for your squeeze page. That doesn't mean long copy that's boring, or long copy just for the sake of being long. It means you must put in the same effort to create a persuasive squeeze page as you would in creating a sales letter for your products and services. Indeed giving up one's name and e-mail address is actually a form of payment.

And your offer to get them to opt in must contain true value. It must be an ethical bribe that, when presented, your prospect would actually pay money for it. It must be a no-brainer to subscribe. These days people can smell junk offers before they're even presented.

Obviously I can't cover every possible way to improve your conversion rate. But I will talk about some copy and persuasion elements that can have a serious impact on your bottom line.

Remember…advertising is salesmanship multiplied. Nothing more. And advertising copy, or copywriting, is salesmanship in print. The purpose of a copywriter's job is to sell. Period. The selling is accomplished by persuasion with the written word, much like a television commercial sells (if done properly) by persuading with visuals and audio. And this fact holds true whether you're selling a $5,000 seminar or merely selling them into providing their name and email address.

FOCUS ON THEM, NOT YOU

When a prospect reads your name squeeze page, the one thing he will be wondering from the start is: "what's in it for me?"

And if your copy doesn't tell him, he'll click away to another website faster than he can read the headline or lead.

A lot of marketers make this mistake. They focus on them as a company. How long they've been in business, who their biggest customers are, how they've spent ten years of research and millions of dollars on developing this product, blah, blah.

Actually, those points are important. But they should be expressed in a way that matters to your potential customer. Remember, once he's left your site, you've lost a subscriber!

When writing your copy, it helps to think of it as writing a letter to an old friend. In fact, I often picture a friend of mine who most closely fits my prospect's profile. What would I say to convince this friend to subscribe to my list? How would I target my friend's objections and beliefs to help *my cause?*

When you're writing to a friend, you'll use the pronouns "I" and "you." When trying to convince your friend, you might say: "Look, I know you think you've tried every widget out there. But you should know that…"

And it goes beyond just writing in the second person. That is, addressing your prospect as "you" within the copy. The fact of the matter is there are many successful ads that *weren't* written in the second person. Some are written in the first person perspective, where the writer uses "I." Other times the third person is used, with "she," "he," and "them."

And even if you *do* write in the second person, it doesn't necessarily mean your copy is about them. For example:

> "As a real estate agent, <u>you</u> can take comfort in the fact that I've sold over 10,000 homes and mastered the tricks of the trade"

Although you're writing in the second person, you're really still focusing on yourself.

So how *can* you focus on them? Glad you asked. One way is to…

EMPHASIZE BENEFITS, NOT FEATURES

What are features? They are descriptions of what qualities a product possesses.

- The XYZ car delivers 55 miles per gallon in the city.
- Our ladder's frame is made from a lightweight durable steel alloy.
- Our glue is protected by a patent.
- This database has a built-in data-mining system.

And what are benefits? They are what those features mean to your prospects.

- You'll save money on gas *and* cut down on environmental pollutants when you use our energy saving high-performance hybrid car. Plus, you'll feel the extra *oomph* when you're passing cars, courtesy of the efficient electric motor, which *they don't have!*

- Lightweight durable steel-alloy frame means you'll be able to take it with you with ease, and use it in places most other ladders can't go, while still supporting up to 800 pounds. No more backaches lugging around that heavy ladder. And it'll last for 150 years, so you'll never need to buy another ladder again!

- Patent-protected glue ensures you can use it on wood, plastic, metal, ceramic, glass, and tile…without messy cleanup and without ever having to re-glue it again—guaranteed!

- You can instantly see the "big picture" hidden in your data, _and_ pull the most arcane statistics on demand. Watch your business do a "180" in no time flat, when you instantly know why it's failing in the first place! It's all done with our built-in data-mining system that's so easy to use, my twelve year-old son used it successfully _right out of the box._

I just made up those examples, but I think you understand my point. By the way, did you notice in the list of features where I wrote "steel alloy?" But in the benefits I wrote "steel-alloy" (with a hyphen). Not sure off-hand which one is correct, but I know which one I'd use. Here's why: you are not writing to impress your English teacher or win any awards. The only award you're after is your copy beating the control (control being the best-selling copy so far), so take some liberty in grammar, punctuation, and sentence structure. You want it to be read and acted upon, not read and admired! But—back to benefits…

If you were selling an expensive watch, you wouldn't tell your reader that the face is 2 inches in diameter and the band is made of leather. You _show_ him how the extra-large face will tell him the time at a glance. No sir! He won't have to squint and look foolish to everyone around him trying to read this magnificent timepiece. And how about the way he'll project success and charisma when he wears the beautiful gold watch with its handcrafted custom leather band? How his lover will find him irresistible when he's all dressed up to go out, wearing the watch. Or how the watch's status and beauty will attract the ladies.

Incidentally, did you notice how I brought up *not squinting* as a benefit? Does that sound like a silly benefit? Not if you are selling to affluent baby boomers suffering from degrading vision. They probably hate it when someone they're trying to impress sees them squint in order to read something. It's all part of their inner desire, which you need to discover. And which even *they* may not know about. That is, until you show them a better way.

The point is to address the benefits of the product, not its features. And when you do that, you're focusing on your reader and his interests, his desires. The trick is to highlight those specific benefits (and word them correctly) that push your reader's emotional hot buttons. How do you do that? Read on!

PUSH THEIR EMOTIONAL HOT BUTTONS

This is where research really pays off. Because in order to push those buttons, you need to first know what they are.

Listen to this story first, and I'll tell you what I mean: Once upon a time a young man walked into a Chevrolet dealer's showroom to check out a Chevy Camaro. He had the money, and he was ready to make a buying decision. But he couldn't decide if he wanted to buy the Camaro or the Ford Mustang up the road at the Ford dealer.

A salesman approached him and soon discovered the man's dilemma.

"Tell me what you like best about the Camaro," said the salesman.

"It's a _fast_ car. I like it for its speed."

After some more discussion, the salesman learned the man had just started dating a cute college cheerleader. So what did the salesman do?

Simple. He changed his pitch accordingly, to push the hot buttons he knew would help advance the sale. He told the man about how impressed his new girlfriend would be _when he came home with this car!_ He placed the mental image in the man's mind of he and his girlfriend cruising to the beach in the Camaro. How all of his friends will be envious when they see him riding around with a beautiful girl in a beautiful car.

And suddenly the man saw it. He got it. And the salesman recognized this and piled it on even more. Before you know it, the man wrote a nice fat check to the Chevy dealership, because he was *sold!*

The salesman found those hot buttons and pushed them like never before until the man realized he wanted the Camaro more than he wanted his money.

I know what you're thinking...the man said he liked the car because it was fast, didn't he?

Yes, he did. But subconsciously, what he really desired was a car that would impress his girlfriend, his friends, and in his mind make them love him more! In his mind he equated speed with thrill. Not because he wanted an endless supply of speeding tickets, but because he thought that thrill would make him more attractive, more likeable.

Perhaps the man didn't even realize this fact himself. But the salesman sure did. And he knew which emotional hot buttons to press to get the sale.

Now, where does the research pay off? Well, a good salesman knows how to ask the kinds of questions that will tell him which buttons to press on the fly. When you're writing copy, you don't have that luxury. It's therefore very important to know upfront the wants, needs, and desires of your prospects for that very reason. If you haven't done your homework, your prospect is going to decide that he'd rather keep his money than buy your product. Remember, copywriting is **salesmanship in print!**

It's been said many times: <u>People don't like to be sold</u>. But they do like to buy. And they buy based on emotion first and foremost. Then they justify their decision with logic, *even after they are already sold emotionally.* So be sure to back up your emotional pitch with logic to nurture that justification at the end.

And while we're on the subject, let's talk a moment about perceived "hype" in a sales letter. A lot of more "conservative" advertisers have decided that they don't like hype, because they consider hype to be old news, been-there-and-done-that, my customers won't fall for hype, it's not believable anymore.

What they should realize is that hype itself does not sell well. Some less experienced copywriters often try to compensate for their lack of research or not fully understanding their target market or the product itself by adding tons of adjectives and adverbs and exclamation points and big bold type. Whew! If you do your job right, it's just not needed.

That's not to say some adverbs or adjectives don't have their place...only if they're used sparingly, and only if they *advance the sale.*

But I think you'd agree that backing up your copy with proof and believability will go a lot farther in convincing your prospects than "power words" alone. I say *power words*, because there are certain adverbs and adjectives that *have* been proven to make a difference when they're included. This by itself is not hype. But repeated too often, they become less effective, and they take away (at least in your prospect's mind) from the proof.

Which brings us into our next tip...

INCORPORATING PROOF AND BELIEVABILITY

When your prospect reads your ad, you want to make sure he believes any claims you make about the value you're providing. Because if there's any doubt in his mind, he won't bite, no matter how sweet the deal. In fact, the "too good to be true" mentality will virtually guarantee a lost sale...even if it *is* all true.

So what can you do to increase the *perception* of believability? Because after all, it's the perception you need to address up front. But of course you also must make sure your copy is accurate and truthful.

Here are some tried and tested methods that will help:

- If you're dealing with existing customers who already know you deliver as promised, emphasize that trust. Don't leave it up to them to figure it out. Make them stop, cock their heads, and say, "Oh, yeah. The ABC Company *has* never done me wrong before. I can trust them."

- Include testimonials of satisfied customers. Be sure to put full names and locations, where possible. Remember, "A.S." is a lot less believable than "Andy Sherman, Voorhees, NJ." If you can also include a picture of the customer and/or a professional title, that's even better. It doesn't matter that your testimonials aren't from somebody famous or that your prospect does not know these people personally. If you have enough compelling testimonials, and they're believable, you're much better off than not including them at all.

- Pepper your copy with facts and research findings to support your claims. Be sure to credit all sources, even if the fact is common knowledge, because a neutral source goes a long way towards credibility.

- When the copy is in the form of a letter from a specific individual, including a picture of that person helps. But unlike "traditional" real estate letters and other similar ads, I'd put the picture at the end near your signature, or midway through the copy, rather than at the top where it will

The Six Figure Sales Funnel

detract from your headline. And…if your sales letter *is* from a specific individual, be sure to include his credentials to establish him as an expert in his field (relating to your product or service, of course).

- If applicable, cite any awards or third-party reviews the product or service has received.

- If you've sold a lot of widgets, tell them. It's the old "10 million people can't be wrong" adage (they can be, but your prospect will likely take your side on the matter).

- If you can swing it, adding a celebrity endorsement will always help to establish credibility. Heck, if 'ol honest Abe Lincoln recommended your ezine and backs up your claims, it must be true! Ok, you get the idea, though.

- When it makes sense, use 3rd party testimonials. What are 3rd party testimonials? Here's some examples from some Web site copy I wrote when there weren't many customer testimonials available yet:

"Spyware, without question, is on an exponential rise over the last six months."

The Six Figure Sales Funnel

> \- Alfred Huger, Senior Director of Engineering, Symantec Security Response (maker of Norton security software)

"Simply clicking on a banner ad can install spyware."

> \- Dave Methvin, Chief Technology Officer, PC Pitstop

A deployment method is to "trick users into consenting to a software download they think they absolutely need"

> \- Paul Bryan, Director, Security And Technology Unit, Microsoft

Do you see what I did? I took quotes from experts in their respective fields and turned them to my side. But...be sure to get their consent or permission from the copyright holder if there's ever any question about copyrighted materials as your source. Note that I also pushed an emotional hot button: fear. <u>It's been proven that people will generally do more to avoid pain than to obtain pleasure</u>. So why not use that tidbit of info to your advantage?

The Six Figure Sales Funnel

- Reveal a flaw about your product. This helps alleviate the "too good to be true" syndrome. You reveal a flaw that isn't really a flaw. Or reveal a flaw that is minor, just to show that you're being "up front" about your product's shortcomings.

Example: "You're probably thinking right now that this tennis racket is a miracle worker—and it is. But I must tell you that it has one little...shortcoming.

My racket takes about 2 weeks to get used to. In fact, when you first start using it, your game will actually get <u>worse</u>. But if you can just ride it out, you'll see a tremendous improvement in your volleys, net play, serves, ..." And so on.

There's a tendency to think, with all of the ads that we are bombarded with today, that every advertiser is always putting his best foot forward, so to speak. And I think that line of reasoning is accurate, to a point. But isn't it refreshing when someone stands out from the crowd and is honest? In other words, your reader will start to subconsciously believe that you are revealing all of the flaws, even though your best foot *still* stands forward.

- Use "lift notes." These are a brief note or letter from a person of authority. Not necessary a celebrity, although that can add credibility, too. A person of authority is someone well recognized in their field (which is related to your product) that they are qualified to talk about. Lift notes may be a separate web page altogether (i.e. opens in a new window), part of the copy itself, or even in the form of a popover window. As always, test!

- If you are limiting the offer with a deadline "order by" date, be sure the deadline is real and does not change. Deadline dates that change every day are sure to reduce credibility. The prospect will suspect, "if his deadline date keeps changing, he's not telling the truth about it...I wonder what else he's not telling the truth about."

- Avoid baseless "hype." I discussed that in my previous tip. Enough said.

THE UNIQUE SELLING PROPOSITION (USP)

Also known as the unique selling *position*, the USP is often one of the most oft-misunderstood elements of a good sales letter. It's what separates your product or service from your competitors. Let's take a quick look at some unique selling propositions for a product itself:

1)   **Lowest Price** – If you've got the corner marketed on budget prices, flaunt it. Wal-Mart has made this USP famous lately, but it's not new to them. In fact, selling for cheaper has been around as long as capitalism itself. Personally, I'm not crazy about price wars, because someone can always come along and sell for cheaper. Then it's time for a new strategy...

2)   **Superior Quality** – If it outperforms your competitor's product or is made with higher quality materials, it's a good bet that you could use this fact to your advantage. For example, compare Breyers Ice Cream to their competitor's. From the packaging to the wholesome superior ingredients, the quality is evident. It may cost a little more than their

competitor's ice cream, but for their market, it sells.

3)   **Superior Service** – If you offer superior service over your competitor's, people will buy from you instead. This is especially true with certain markets that are all about service: long-distance, Internet service providers, cable television, etc.

4)   **Exclusive Rights** – My favorite! If you can legitimately claim that your product is protected by a patent or copyright, licensing agreement, etc., then you have a winner for exclusive rights. If you have a patent, even the *President of the U.S.* <u>must</u> buy it from you.

Ok, what if your product or service is no different than your competitor's? I would disagree, because there are always differences. The trick is to turn them into a positive advantage for you. You want to put your "best foot forward." So what can we do in this scenario?

One way is to present something that your company has devised internally that no other company does. Look, there's a reason why computer store "A" offers to beat their competitor's price for the same product by X%. If you look closely, the two packages are never exactly the same. Company "B" offers a free scanner, while company "A" offers a free printer. Or some other difference. They are comparing apples to oranges. So unless you find a company with the exact same package (you won't...they've seen to that), you won't be able to cash in.

But what if you truly have the same widget for sale as the guy up the road?

Unless your prospect knows the inner workings of both your and your competitor's product, including the manufacturing process, customer service, and everything in-between, then you have a little potential creative licensing here. But you must be truthful.

For example, if I tell my readers that my product is bathed in steam to ensure purity and cleanliness (like the cans and bottles in most beer manufacturing processes), it doesn't matter that Joe's Beer up the road does the same thing. That fact that Joe doesn't advertise this fact makes it a USP in your prospect's eyes.

Want some more USP examples?

- We are the only car repair shop that will *buy your car* if you are not 100 percent satisfied with our work.

- Delivered in 30 minutes or it's on us!

- No other furniture company will pay for your shipping.

- Our recipe is so secret, only three people in the world know it!

As with most ways to boost copy response, research is the key with your USP. Sometimes your USP is obvious, for example if you have a patent. Other times you must do a little legwork to discover it (or shape it to your target market).

Here's where a little persistence and in-person selling really pays off. Let me give you an example to illustrate what I mean:

Suppose your company sells beanbag chairs for kids. So you, being the wise marketer that you are, decide to sell these beanbags in person to prospects before writing your copy. After completing twenty different pitches for your product, you discover that 75 percent of those you visited asked if the chair would eventually leak. Since the chairs are for kids, it's only logical that parents would be concerned about their youngster jumping on it, rolling on it, and doing all things possible to break the seam and "spill the beans."

So when you write your copy, you make sure you address that issue: "You can rest assure that our super-strong beanbag chairs are triple-stitched for guaranteed leak-proof performance. No other company will make this guarantee about their beanbag chairs!"

THE HEADLINE

If you're going to make a single change to boost your response rate the most, focus on your headline (you *do* have one, don't you?).

Why? Because <u>five times</u> as many people read your headline than your copy. Quite simply, a headline is…an ad for your ad. People won't stop their busy lives to read your copy unless you give them a good reason to do so. So a good headline promises some news and a benefit.

Perhaps you're thinking, "What's this about news, you say?"

Think about the last time you browsed through your local newspaper. You checked out the articles, one by one, and occasionally an ad may have caught your eye. Which ads were the ones most likely to catch your eye?

The ones that looked like an article, of course.

The ones with the headline that promised news. The ones with fonts and type that closely resembled the fonts and type used in articles. The ones that were placed where articles were placed (as opposed to being placed on a full page of ads, for example).

And the ones with the most compelling headlines that convinced you it's worth a few minutes to read the copy.

The headline is *that* powerful and *that* important.

I've seen many ads over the years that didn't even *have* a headline. And that's just silly. It's the equivalent of flushing good money spent on advertising right down the toilet.

Why? Because your response can increase dramatically by not only adding a headline, but by making that headline almost impossible to resist *for your target market*.

And those last three words are important. *Your target market*.

For example, take a look at the following headline:

Announcing...New High-Tech Gloves Protect Wearer Against Hazardous Waste

News, and a benefit.

Will that headline appeal to everyone?

No, and you don't care about everyone. But for someone who handles hazardous waste, they would sure appreciate knowing about this little gem.

That's your target market, and it's your job to get them to read your ad. Your headline is the way you do that.

Ok, now where do you find great headlines? You look at other successful ads (especially direct response) that have stood the test of time. You look for ads that run regularly in magazines and other publications. How do you know they're good? Because if they didn't do their job, the advertiser wouldn't keep running them again and again.

You get on the mailing lists of the big direct response companies like Agora and Boardroom and save their direct mail packages. You read the National Enquirer.

Huh? You heard that correctly. The National Enquirer has some of the best headlines in the business. Pick up a recent issue and you'll see what I mean. Ok, now how could you adapt some of those headlines to your own product or service?

Your headline should create a sense of urgency. It should be as specific as possible (i.e. say $1,007,274.23 instead of "a million dollars").

The headline appearance is also very important. Make sure the type used is bold and large, and different from the type used in the copy. Generally, longer headlines tend to out pull shorter ones, even when targeting more "conservative" prospects.

Some other sites online where you can get great headlines (from master copywriter John Carlton, no less) are:

- http://www.otsdirect.com/products.html

- http://www.trsdirect.com/product.php

- http://www.ohpdirect.com/product.php

On each page, click on the individual products in order to view the ads and headlines.

It should go without saying that when you use other successful headlines, you adapt them to your own product or service. Never copy a headline (or any other written copyrighted piece of work for that matter) word for word. Copywriters and ad agencies are notoriously famous for suing for plagiarism. And rightfully so.

THE MORE YOU TELL, THE MORE YOU SELL

The debate on using long copy versus short copy never seems to end. Usually it is a newcomer to copywriting who seems to think that long copy is boring and, well…long. "I would never read that much copy," they say.

The truth is, long versus short is relative, and consistent testing has shown that longer copy tends to out-pull shorter copy. Of course, there are always exceptions, and your own test results should be the deciding factor.

The person who says he would never read all that copy is making a big mistaking in copywriting: he is going with his gut reaction instead of relying on test

The Six Figure Sales Funnel

results. He is thinking that he himself is the prospect. He's not. We're never our own prospects.

There have been many studies and split tests conducted on the long copy versus short copy debate. And the clear winner is always long copy. But that's targeted relevant long copy as opposed to untargeted boring long copy.

Some significant research has found that readership tends to fall off dramatically at around 300 words, but does not drop off again until around 3,000 words.

If I'm selling an expensive set of golf clubs and send my long copy to a person who's plays golf occasionally, or always wanted to try golf, I am sending my sales pitch to the wrong prospect. It is not targeted effectively. And so if a person who receives my long copy doesn't read past the 300th word, they weren't qualified for my offer in the first place. It wouldn't have mattered whether they read up to the 100th word or 10,000[th] word. They still wouldn't have made a purchase.

However, if I sent my long copy to an avid die-hard golfer, who just recently purchased other expensive golf products through the mail, painting an irresistible offer, telling him how my clubs will knock 10 strokes off his game, he'll likely read every word. And if I've targeted my message correctly, he will buy.

Remember, if your prospect is 3000 miles away, it's not easy for him to ask you a question. You must anticipate and answer all of his questions and overcome all objections in your copy if you are to be successful.

And make sure you don't throw everything you can think of under the sun in there. You only need to include as much information as you need to make the sale...and not one word more. If it takes a 10-page sales letter (when printed out), so be it. If it takes a 16-page one, fine. But if the 10-page sales letter tests better than the 16-page one, then by all means go with the winner.

Does that mean every prospect must read every word of your copy before he will order your product? Of course not. Some will read every word and then go back and reread it again. Some will read the headline and lead, then skim much of the body and land on the close. Some will scan the entire body, then go back and read it. All of those prospects may end up purchasing the offer, but they also all may have different styles of reading and skimming.

Which brings us to the next tip...

WRITE TO BE SCANNED

Your layout is very important in a sales letter, because you want your letter to look inviting, refreshing to the eyes. In short, you want your prospect to stop what he's doing and read your letter.

If he sees a letter with tiny margins, no indentations, no breaks in the text, no white space, and no subheads...if he sees a page of nothing but densely-packed words, do you think he'll be tempted to read it? Not likely.

If you do have ample white space and generous margins, short sentences, short paragraphs, subheads, and an italicized or underlined word here and there for emphasis, it will certainly look more inviting to read.

When reading your letter, some prospects will start at the beginning and read word for word. Some will read the headline and maybe the lead, then read the "P.S." at the end of the letter and see who the letter is from, then start from the beginning.

And some folks will scan through your letter, noticing the various subheads strategically positioned by you throughout your letter, then decide if it's worth their time to read the entire thing. Some may never read the entire letter, but order anyways.

You must write for all of them. Interesting and compelling long copy for the studious reader, and short paragraphs and sentences, white space, and subheads for the skimmer.

Subheads are the smaller headlines sprinkled throughout your copy.

Like this.

When coming up with your headline, some of the headlines that didn't make the cut can make great subheads. A good subhead forces your prospect to keep reading, threading him along from start to finish throughout your copy, while also providing the glue necessary to keep skimmers skimming.

THE STRUCTURE OF AIDAS

There's a well-known structure in successful sales letters, described by the acronym *AIDA*.

AIDA stands for:

- **A**ttention
- **I**nterest
- **D**esire
- **A**ction

First, you capture your prospect's attention. This is done with your headline and lead. If your ad fails to capture your prospect's attention, it fails completely. Your prospect doesn't read your stellar copy, and doesn't order your product or service.

Then you want to build a strong interest in your prospect. You want him to keep reading, because if he reads, he just might buy.

Next, you channel a desire. Having a targeted market for this is key, because you're not trying to create a desire where one did not already exist. You want to capitalize on an existing desire, which your prospect *may or may not know he already has.* And you want your prospect to experience that desire for your product or service.

Finally, you present a call to action. You want him to pick up the telephone, return the reply card, attend the sales presentation, order your product, whatever. You need to ask for the sale (or response, if that's the goal). You don't want to beat around the bush at this point. If your letter and AIDA structure is sound and persuasive, here's where you present the terms of your offer and urge the prospect to act now.

A lot has been written about the AIDA copywriting formula. I'd like to add one more letter to the acronym: *S for Satisfy.*

In the end, after the sale is made, you want to satisfy your prospect, who is now a customer. You want to deliver exactly what you promised (or even more), by the date you promised, in the manner you promised. In short, you want to give him every reason in the world to trust you the next time you sell him a back-end offer. And of course you'd rather he doesn't return the product (although if he does, you also execute your return policy *as promised*).

Either way, you want your customers to be satisfied. It will make you a lot more money in the long run.

And Finally...

The Six Figure Sales Funnel

Great copy is made, not born. It is derived from proven test results designed to do one thing and do it well: sell.

Effective advertising doesn't always use "grammatically correct" English. It uses short sentences, fragments. Like this. It convinces you to buy, and buy now. Period.

It talks about benefits, not features. It sells on emotion and reinforces the decision to buy with logic.

It paints a compelling picture and irresistible offer that forces your prospect to act and act now! And if it doesn't, then you drop that ad like a hot potato and go with one that does.

Effective persuasion is like your top salesperson--the one who continues to break all your sales records year after year--on the job 24 x 7, multiplied by thousands or millions! Just imagine if that salesperson, the one with proven results, could be multiplied as much as you wanted.

Now that would be effective (and cost-efficient) marketing!

And that's the kind of proven marketing I'm talking about here.

CONCLUSION

I hope these examples have helped you to develop the mindset to be on the lookout for opportunities everywhere. I've tried to arrange these ideas in a logical format, so you can print this report out and go through each one with a highlighter and pen, making notes, and adding your own thoughts.

There's a great quote: *"More occurs from movement than will ever happen from meditation and contemplation."* And so I would strongly urge you to take action. Don't just read this and put it on a shelf or bury it on your computer's hard drive. Read it. Use it. Own it.

Take action and reap the rewards. To your great success!